FLESH AND BONES

SERMONS

BY THE REV. DR.
A. K. M. ADAM

Wipf and Stock Publishers
150 West Broadway • Eugene OR 97401
2001

Printed by Wipf and Stock Publishers, 2001
ISBN: 1-57910-767-2

Text set in ITC Galliard

Titles set in Diehl Deco by Marley Diehl & Apostrophe,
used by their kind permission

This collection © A. K. M. Adam
All proceeds from the sale of this collection go
for the benefit of St. Luke's Parish, Evanston

The sermon published here as "Seminary Baccalaureate" was first published as "Crossing Over, Pressing On," in the *Princeton Seminary Bulletin* 19/3 (1998), 236-241, and is reprinted with their kind permission.

CONTENTS

Preface	1
2 Epiphany	4
Proper 8	9
Transfiguration	13
Proper 9	17
Requiem	22
Proper 28	25
3 Advent	29
Proper 15	33
1 Christmas	37
Holy Name	41
Proper 12	45
7 Easter	50
4 Advent	54
4 Lent	58

2 Lent	62
Pentecost	66
Proper 7	71
World AIDS Day	75
Good Friday	82
Easter Sunday	85
6 Easter	90
Seminary Baccalaureate	95
Easter Vigil	101

PREFACE

Preaching is a fundamentally presumptuous gesture. The stakes are so high—in a very real sense, we preachers put ourselves in the place of prophets, evangelists, apostles, perhaps even articulating Jesus' words in our own awkward speech. How can we summon up the gall to represent the Word with our mortal tongues? What nerve justifies standing up and preaching about sin, about AIDS, about discipleship, life, and death?

The presumption seems all the more striking when sermons, which presented orally can at least call upon inflection, intonation, personal acquaintance, and evanescence to obscure their poverty, then appear in bare printed words. "Oh dear, did I really say *that*?" Sermons, by their role in life, should be consumed (aurally), digested (spiritually), and left behind (definitely); yet here they come again.

They come again with fond memories of all who have, by their patience and grace and encouragement, brought these sermons to life. As Margaret and I read through my files to cull out the sermons worth compiling for this collection, I met innumerable old friends again. "Where on earth is Fuquay-Varina?" Margaret asked, or "Do you remember St. Albans's?"

I did remember where Fuquay-Varina was, roughly (it's in North Carolina, about 50 miles south of Durham), and after some coaching I could call to mind St. Alban's (St. Petersburg Beach). But especially I remembered the kind people who sat still and offered encouraging words as I learned something about preaching. Congregations have taught me a good deal more about preaching than did my seminary professors (not because of any shortcomings in Harry Adams's or Bill Muehl's instruction!). While I quail to think about those first few ventures in preaching at a tiny mission in Pittsburgh, it's the love and openness of the congregations I've served that have made all these sermons possible. If there is anything good, anything worthwhile, anything edifying, anything comforting, anything true in these words, think of the great souls who have elicited them from me. These sermons were preached in a wide variety of settings: at St. Luke's Parish, Evanston; St. James's Church, Tampa (since then, merged with House of Prayer, Tampa); Trinity Church, Princeton; St. Thomas's, Snell Isle; the Cathedral of St. Peter, St. Petersburg; St. Michael's Church, Trinity Cathedral, and St. Matthias's Church, Trenton; Princeton Theological Seminary; Christ Church, New Brunswick; All Saints' Church, Tarpon Springs; and Nassau Presbyterian Church, Princeton. These congregations made possible anything good in the sermons collected here, and I thank them with all my heart for inviting me into their quarters in the household of God. I should likewise thank the staff of the NAMES Foundation in San Francisco, who welcomed me to spend a semester poring over panel after panel of the AIDS Memorial Quilt, and to Princeton Theological Seminary for a grant to support that research.

Every day I realize more forcefully how deeply my mother and father affected my relation to language; from them I learned to love words with an unquenchable passion, to relish the painstaking attention to detail that seeks precisely the right word, that orders those words deliberately into clauses, that obliges a writer to stay up all night correcting and editing rather than offer a second-rate composition. Playing Scrabble with my mother, capping couplets with my father, learning why "Aliquippa" and "McKee's Rocks" are funny while "Lawrenceville" and "Oakland" aren't—all of these set the stage for how I've learned to preach. It is, to a great extent, their doing.

By the time I started preaching, though, they were less prominent in my daily life than my beloved Margaret. She has been a brutally fierce critic, and an unwaveringly enthusiastic supporter. Indeed, this collection is largely her work—from the idea to the selection to the editing to the order in which they appear. Margaret has shaped my theology daily for more than twenty years, and these words (and the cameo appearances she makes in these sermons) make only a wan acknowledgment of her influence on all I do.

Finally, a word about St. Luke's Parish, for whose benefit we put together this collection. St. Luke's path and mine converged at mutually tumultuous and, I dare say, not propitious circumstances; the joy I have known in serving St.Luke's bespeaks God's power to relocate mountains and transform evil to good. While I gladly handed over the responsibilities of leadership to Virgil Robinson and Charles Caskey, I will never yield the glorious privilege of having taken part in the life of such a marvelous congregation.

2 EPIPHANY

Isaiah 62:1-5; 1 Corinthians 12:1-11; John 2:1-11

For Zion's sake I will not keep silent, and for Jerusalem's sake I will not rest, until her vindication shines out like the dawn, and her salvation like a burning torch. The nations shall see your vindication, and all the kings your glory.

In the Name of God Almighty, the Blessed Trinity— *Amen.*

Which transmits light better: dirt or flesh?

That's not just an idle question. You see, I was listening to the radio the other day, and I heard a program about Science Fairs. One caller wanted to know how much parental help was appropriate, and another wanted ideas for her daughter's project, and another caller had a complaint about judging practices. And because I had important things to accomplish, and really very little time to accomplish them in, I was listening to this radio program about Science Fairs in rapt fascination.

But not exactly *listening*, for as I was listening I found myself *daydreaming* about a world in which parents and children put hours of time into their Theology Fair projects. Imagine that! — a world where little Rupert might spend weeks studying monastic spirituality, and would then put together a report on the evolution of the variety of non-Eucharistic liturgies in the Catholic tradition. Or Annabelle might conduct field research on how Christian theology might look if the Protevangelium of James had been incorporated into the New Testament. Moms and Dads would offer encouragement and advice, we'd have a big display over at Pierce Hall, and Fr. Smith could give handsome participation prizes for all concerned, and we could send on one or two exemplary projects to the diocesan Theology Fair.

And as I was daydreaming about this fantasy world, someone called in the radio program and explained that his son was preparing a Science Fair project on which transmitted light better: dirt or flesh. The youth in question was going to get a strong light and beam it at varying quantities of soil and hamburger meat. Now, I experienced a shiver of vegetarian dismay about *that* proposal, but in an instant I had a revelation that this, indeed, was the whole problem that had been lurking in the back of my mind through the whole Theology Fair reverie: how well does flesh transmit light?

You see, the authorities who were pitching Science Fairs to me over the radio kept stressing that the pivotal thing, the decisive point which made Science Fair projects valuable as a learning experience for our children, was the degree to which children perceived their parents supporting and valuing their work. If children could see that Mom and Dad were impressed, were encouraging, were positive about putting effort into learning about science—*not* just about winning, thank you very much—if a child's project engaged her parents in a shared sense of pride and discovery, then it was an irreplaceable learning experience, one that would frequently lead to a lifelong appreciation for scientific knowledge.

The teacher part of my brain said that was exactly right. We can say what we want about the value of learning, or about the importance of experimental science, but if our children don't see that importance reflected in our willingness to devote time and effort and enthusiasm to their own work, they will recognize that our rhetoric of support as superficial and sterile.

And that's how I was dreaming about a Theology Fair. How many of us can say that our children or our best friends can see in our lives a commitment to the importance of Christian ethical practices? Can they see light through our flesh? Can they see God's justice in our actions, God's truth in our lives?

I've been around long enough to know that it's easier to shine when there's an intense fire close by; it's easier for us to live as honest disciples of Jesus when we're close by people who blaze with God's glory. It's easier to catch some of the glow from our sisters or brothers and reflect it on to the world. But we're not called only to pass along the light of the saints. It's Epiphany; it's the season for doing a little shining ourselves. It's a reminder that when the truth of the gospel comes into our lives, *it makes a difference*. When you taste the water, now become wine, you know that something has happened here. When your children and neighbors see that some transformation has taken place, however subtle, however gradual, some unmistakable transformation has taken place, then they recognize a commitment that runs deeper than attendance on Sunday morning and writing a check.

Shine a little of that light. Show a little of that glory.

Now, I have a particular advantage when it comes to perceiving God's people shine. All I have to do is remove my glasses, and everyone in I see is suffused with a soft, warm radiance. But the shining I'm talking about this morning isn't a simple soft-focus glow; I'm asking you to commit yourselves to the kind of radiance that takes hard work. I'm thinking of people like my friends in Florida, whom I miss very much, who take hours and weeks and months of their time planning a series of retreats for people affected by AIDS. They literally plan their year around these retreats, and when we all come together and reach out and pray with the retreatants and with each other, my friends *glow*. These friends aren't pasteboard saints. Indeed, many of them are unwelcome in most churches, and some of them can be terribly difficult to work with. But when we put our hands together to serve our sisters and brothers, God's light shines through them.

Remember that the lesson this morning doesn't say, "It's a good idea in principle to follow God's ways." Or it doesn't say, "It's a nice gift for God when we choose to behave in particularly holy ways." The Old Testament lesson says, "That's for *us*"—Isaiah tells his friends, "For *Zion's* sake I will not keep silent; for *Jerusalem's* sake I will not rest." It's for our own good that we are called to live in ways that find in a watered-down world, the blessed wine of God's presence. Because we know that, for the most part, we live apart from that light; we know that it is twilight, it is evening, and apart from Christ it gets gloomier and gloomier. Apart from God's light, we are Desolate; we are Forsaken when we turn away from God. If we turn away from this light, we are lost; we don't know where we're going; we're as helpless as if we were in a basement room at midnight and the bulb burned out.

In the twilight, in the cold, it takes hard work to get a fire going. It takes a lot of effort to coax an ember along into an flame. There are many people out there like the earnest seminarian who said, "Whenever I see a glimmering spark of the Spirit, I want to nurture and water it." There are a lot of people out there who—whether well-intentioned or hostile—are trying to water our sparks, making it hard to keep that glimmer alive. And it can be especially challenging to folks like many of us, who are well-scrubbed, comfortable, fairly bright, people who already look like a crown of beauty in the hand of the Lord, and a royal diadem in the hand of our God. People who are doing all right in the world have a hard time realizing that their finery may conceal a Desolate and Forsaken soul. Some bright minds are the dimly burning wicks. This is a chilly, dark world, where true light is rare, and if there are occasional bonfires along the road, there are many more stretches where midnight has fallen hard, and where even the dreamers dream only of bleak obscurity.

So we have to keep the spark alive, we've got to pass it along to our children, we've got to show it to the world around us. Our job, our vocation is to carry God's fire outside these walls, to those who sit in darkness, to those who are chilled to the bone. We are called to gather here on the Lord's Day, so that the spark in each of us can flourish in the warmth we share. We are called to *go out*, then, and carry that flame, even if it's a sputtering, hesitant flame, out to our sisters and brothers. We are called to follow Jesus *visibly, inconveniently,* to let our light out of the bushel and to let it shine *through our flesh.*

It would be great to have a Theology Fair in Pierce Hall, with banners and reporters and video cameras and the Archbishop of Canterbury to judge projects, with enthusiastic children and proud, supportive parents. It would be great if we were actually informed and concerned about the contemporary influence of Arian christology. But as long as there are lonely hearts, hungry bellies, broken souls, we can better spread the light and the warmth of the gospel by making time to reach out to our sisters and brothers. If our children can see us serving others in the name of Jesus, we will be transmitting the light. If our neighbors know that we are not too busy to make time for daily prayer, we'll be radiating. If we honor our faith by serving God before we serve ourselves, then the nations will see God's justice, and the whole world will glimpse God's glory; we will shine with the radiance of Christ's glory, that he may be known and worshiped to the ends of the earth—and our flesh will transmit God's light very well indeed.

PROPER 8

1 Kings 19:15-16, 19-21; Galatians 5:1, 13-25; Luke 9:51-62

If we live by the Spirit, let us also be guided by the Spirit.

In the Name of God: Father, Son and Holy Spirit— *Amen.*

There was a time in my life when I didn't want to follow Jesus. There was a time in my life when the very last thing I ever wanted was to have anything at all to do with the man who got the churches started, who was responsible for ministers dressing up in silly clothing, for children putting on uncomfortable shoes on Sundays, for the commercialism of Christmas and the hypocrisy of Easter. I looked to Jesus, but all I saw was baloney. I didn't *need* Jesus, I didn't have any use for anyone who *did* need Jesus, and I could see, plain as the noses on our faces, that this whole enterprise, from the so-called resurrection down to today, was a sorry refuge for weak-minded wishful thinkers who didn't have the strength to face life without an invisible Daddy promising to make everything better for them in a pie-in-the-sky future life. I was a skeptic, and I meant business about it.

I can't tell you exactly what happened; no blinding light, no voice from heaven. I *could* tell you a lot of small stories; most of them involve my beloved wife Margaret in one way or another, Margaret and her family. But I can't tell you about God appearing to me from heaven and slapping me upside my head, or Elijah coming and tossing a cloak onto me, and me then dropping my plow and following. That's partly because I just didn't know what was happening to me even as it was happening; God was working on me in ways I couldn't spell out at the time, and I still can't spell them out. But I think it's mostly because God's way is usually not to do things with spotlights and special effects, but instead to manage the tiny details in such a way that things just *happen* in the right way. The God who bent my will from defiance and skepticism to submission and faith didn't bludgeon me, didn't beat me with a stick to change my mind, but just set me up to change my own mind.

The reason I bring this up this morning—apart from a general inclination to tell you all stories about myself—is that I take it that this is close to what St. Paul says about being "led by the Spirit." When Israel wandered throught he wilderness, they had a pillar of cloud by day and a pillar of fire by night, but we don't usually get such obvious road signs in our lives. And for us, just as for the Galatians, some of the most obvious signals that we get come from our bodies; we tend to be led by our flesh. We get clear and distinct signals from our fleshly existence for when we're hungry, when we're thirsty, when we need to rest, and various other activities. We also get signals, less clear but often just as urgent, which have to do with the more subtle needs we have. In many ways, I'm a very physical person; I need to express what I'm thinking by what I do. If I feel very affectionate, I want to hug someone; if I feel very angry, I want to break something. I want my muscles and skin and bones and nerves to do their part in talking out what's on my mind. This is another way of being led by the flesh; and because the flesh is not very good at subtle reasoning, we need to *restrain* ourselves from acting indiscriminately on the impulse of our bodily urges.

Probably the least effective way of resisting the impulses of the flesh relies on thinking hard about what's best for us. Our flesh is strong enough and subtle enough to warp our thinking, to help us rationalize practically anything we want to do. When we try to restrain the flesh by laws, by rules, we have to back up our rules with punishments, a kind of reasoning the flesh understands all too well—but punishment isn't a godly way of restraining our impulses. In important ways, punishment is *complicit* with desire; punishment, as it were, *ratifies* the object we desire as something desirable, and uses force to combat that longing.

But when St. Paul reminds us that we are not to be led by the flesh, but rather to be led by the Spirit, he is urging us not to torture ourselves with punishments; he recognizes that the holier way to overcome temptation is to lose the temptation in the first place. "For what the flesh desires is opposed to the Spirit, and what the Spirit desires is opposed to the flesh; for these are opposed to each other, to prevent you from doing what you want. But if you are led by the Spirit, you are not subject to the law." If you are led by the Spirit, the law doesn't have any bearing on you. You don't need the law any more than you need a woolen overcoat in Florida. You don't need the law, because the Spirit is leading you into the right ways. My family occasionally goes out to Halo Pub to get ice cream on summer weeknights, and when we do I usually just have a cup of coffee. It's not that I don't like ice cream—far from it—but I realized that if I didn't lose the temptation to eat vast amounts of ice cream, I would have something more *weighty* to lose.

Paul urges us not to be led by the flesh, but to be led by the Spirit. When he says that, he doesn't just mean always choosing to do good deeds (though he surely hopes and expects that Spirit-led people will behave better than people who are led by the flesh). Being led by the Spirit means changing the way you decide about where you're going; it means tuning in to a *different* channel for information about the world, about yourself, about what people ought to do. If we are led by the Spirit, we just have different priorities about life. Where we used to enjoy days of licentiousness, drunkenness, carousing, strife, jealousy, and so on, now we look for love, joy, peace, patience, kindness, gentleness, self-control. These ideals don't just enter our lives on signs in big letters, though—it's not a "just say no" affair for most of us. Instead, these ideals seep into our lives when we see other folks whom we respect living by their ideals. We think of self-control instead of excess because we see that admirable, grace-filled women and men are inclined to exercise self-control; we honor peace and gentleness when we see the conflict between patient dignity and violent hatred through the example of a truly great person. When we open our hearts to this message of faith and hope, we begin to be guided by the Spirit of Holiness.

The scary thing about these ways of living is that they can be very hard to tell apart, especially if you're stuck in one or the other. I *do* have an ice cream sometimes; is there a real difference between enjoying an occasional sundae and being led by the flesh's longing for cones? I believe there is such a difference, but the difference comes not in grand ways, with pillars of cloud or angels with fiery swords; the difference doesn't come by making rules against ice cream. Instead, the difference comes from learning to change your habits, your interests, your will in a number of small ways. It can happen suddenly; we all know that God turns some folks' hearts in sudden and dramatic ways. But it can also happen gradually, slowly, from tiny day-to-day changes. Things just start happening, and one day, you've gone from being an irreverent skeptic like me to being a member of the vestry; you've changed from one of those characters who says, "God give me chastity and moderation, but not just yet," to one of the apostles who just follows the Lord everywhere. You will have been led by the Spirit, guided by the Spirit, set free from the law, for which we all give thanks to God.

TRANSFIGURATION

Exodus 34:29-35; Psalm 99; 2 Peter 1:13-21; Luke 9:28-36

We did not follow cleverly devised myths when we made known to you the power and coming of our Lord Jesus Christ, but we had been eyewitnesses of his majesty.

In the Name of God Almighty, the Blessed Trinity— *Amen.*

I have stopped drawing lines in the sand. It doesn't work; I've found that when I get stuck in an argument with someone I know to be dreadfully wrong-headed, or when I build a Maginot Line to protect the inviolable truth I espouse, it turns out that I've overlooked some detail, or someone has a story I hadn't heard. Worst of all, those who *win* their wars against foolishness or tyranny or closed-mindedness show a marked propensity to transform themselves into the mirror images of the cause they're resisting. People resort to violence in protest against violence; people narrow-mindedly insist that everyone share their broad-minded outlook; people denounce superstitious credulity, but in so doing they fall into oversimplified myths their own selves.

This morning, for instance, some proportion of preachers are reflecting on the miraculous incandescence of our Lord and Savior Jesus Christ. They highlight the uniqueness of Jesus, made manifest to Peter and James and John by this capacity spontaneously to begin glowing a supernatural dazzling white. Meanwhile, in other congregations, sophisticated Episcopalians snicker that some credulous rubes actually believe that Jesus climbed up a mountain and sparkled. Perhaps they're even making jokes about how many messiahs it takes to change a light bulb, or how they don't care if it rains or freezes as long as they have a glowing Jesus. They offer a perfectly plausible explanation of this phenomenon that doesn't require twenty-first-century Christians to flout the laws of nature.

Some of these sophisticates are wont to accuse their opposite number of *literalism,* as though it were the height of idiocy actually to believe what's written in Scripture. "Whatever it says, it's not meant to be taken *literally,* it's a *metaphor* that refers to any condition of excited or animated conversation." That's the line-in-the-sand trap, though; the second faction criticizes the first for taking the Bible literally, but both factions are assuming that the most relevant part of the story lies in Jesus' luminance. They're just quibbling about how many foot-candles; the conservatives say "1,000,000," and the liberals say "0," but they're both out their with light meters.

At moments like this, one wonders whether our sisters and brothers have even caught up with the first disciples of Jesus, who show up in the gospels as the slow-witted sidekicks, as the point-missers who rarely attain a theological insight more striking than "Duh." The gospels persistently display Peter and his friends latching onto exactly the wrong part of Jesus' message, focusing on the leaven in the bread instead of recognizing the saving abundance of God, or dreading the Sea of Galilee's Perfect Storm rather than giving thanks for the presence of Jesus among them. Many of our arguments about Scripture get no further than Peter's hasty fixation on building tents for Jesus and Moses and Elijah—some of us wanting to build a spectacular shrine for the Transfiguration, and others wanting to dismiss it altogether as the disciple's having eaten too much spicy food before falling asleep.

St. Luke gives us the opportunity, though, to discern something that our debates tend to mask. Luke invites us to stand with Peter and John and James, to witness Jesus transfigured, "the appearance of his face changed, and his clothes became dazzling white," but *not* to get stuck in Peter's misguided fascination with the vision itself. Luke reminds us that Peter didn't know what he was talking about. We mustn't reduce that astonishing moment on the mountaintop to a mere miracle; the transfiguration of Jesus pulls away the veil for a moment, reminds us what the uniformity and routine of daily life conceal, that *no* place or moment is more than a hair's breadth away from the dazzling disclosure of God's glory.

God's glory suffuses Moses' face, when Moses looked only for a few moments on God's back side. God's glory, a mysterious quality that we can neither pin down nor ignore, God's glory fixes our attention on Moses or Jesus or whomever, and we recognize that something more than ordinary is going on here. God's glory doesn't go away somewhere and hide when John the Revelator lays down his pen; God's glory radiates on, manifest in the saints and the martyrs, in spectacular architecture and exquisite music, in the power of friendship, in the sublime beauty of the world that God established. *We have been eyewitnesses of this majesty.* God's glory shimmered faintly to Margaret and me from a friend's father, sparkling in his eyes, diffusing from his very flesh, just weeks before he died; God's glory calms and refreshes us as we gaze out over the breakers on Lake Michigan, beholding the heights and the depths, the fathomless variety of creation; God's glory calls out to us in majesty and harmony, and if we cannot *recognize* the glory of God, the incipient transfiguration of mundane elements into divine verity, then it were better that our tongues fall mute rather than, like Peter, stammer vacuous trivialities. God's glory is given us not so that we can measure it, but so that we may, by God's grace, grow *into* glory ourselves. God's glory awaits us in just the everyday places and materials from which our skeptical friends would banish God, awaits us not as a secret payoff for hard-working belief, but as a the force of truth waiting for us to set it free, to set ourselves free, in the image of the God who draws us ever onward.

The mystery of the glory of God comes into view when we avert our eyes from the banal either-or choice of magical miraculousness-vs.-bare materialism. Our hope for some taste of that glory depends on our not reducing the transfiguration to a mechanical explanation, nor dismissing it as superstitious conjuration; if we must accept *only* those alternatives, we'll miss out on these most abundant revelations of God's glory. Instead, come, seek out God's glory behind the veil of *here, now,* and pass along that glory to a disenchanted world. That extraordinary divine glory that bathed the wondering apostles on the mountaintop lurks also—in differing inflections—in the rhythmic throb of pulsating particles, in the spectroscopic analysis of the

Paschal candle's Easter light, in the ordinariness of our beloved ones' faces, in the very tediousness of the daily routine. The glory of God inhabits everyday life, stealing in, interrupting, startling us. God's glory *flares* and *ripples*, jarring us out of our captivity to the myths of nature or supernature and awakening us to God's presence. Here, *now*, among these wooden pews and oft-repeated words, God's glory dwells in this ordinary bread and unpretentious wine, in St. Luke's Church of all places, in Evanston, Illinois, nourishing hungry hearts with glory's feast, refreshing thirsty souls with living water from the cup of salvation.

For Christ is transfigured this morning, on mountain top, yet also on altar block and in the spirit and sinew of faith's people. So also Moses is transfigured this morning, hidden in the cleft of Mount Sinai, staring at the Holy One's hinder parts, and Elijah is transfigured this morning and taken up in swirling clouds of glory, and you and I are being transfigured, atom by atom, wish by wish, promise by promise, prayer by prayer, being transfigured together into a body that is not *just* like yours or mine, not flabby or petite, buxom or buff, not pallid or tan or ebony. Our true body is a *transfigured* body of glory, of *God's* glory—and you can see that glory in *you*, in *us*, sisters and brothers, I see that glory waxing and spreading and bursting forth in all manner of ways, free from superstition, free from condescension, free from our own presumptuous definitions of who God might be or how God might be known to us—free at last from the chains of our own making, the servitude we impose on ourselves and our soul's sisters and brothers, free at last to carry into the streets the sign of truth, so that all may see our love and our good works, and recognize in our ways of life a radiant intimation of God's love at work.

PROPER 9

Zechariah 9:9-12; Romans 7:21-8:6; Matthew 11:25-30

In the Name of the Triune God,
    who was and is and ever shall be— *Amen.*

I don't have much of an ear for poetry. I did not inherit my full share of poetry appreciation from my mother and father, both of whom have been English teachers. Still, there are some poems which have caught my attention for some reason; John Donne's 14th Sonnet was one of those.

> Batter my heart, three-personed God; for You
> As yet but knock, breathe, shine, and seek to mend;
> That I may rise and stand, o'erthrow me, and bend
> Your force to break, blow burn, and make me new.
> I, like an usurped town, to another due,
> Labor to admit You, but O, to no end.
> Reason, Your viceroy in me, should defend,
> But is captived, and proves weak or untrue.
> Yet dearly I love You, and would be loved fain,
> But am betrothed unto Your enemy.
> Divorce me, untie or break that knot again;
> Take me to You, imprison me, for I
> Except You enthrall me, never shall be free,
> Nor ever chaste, except You ravish me.

Though I once loved the contrasts, the paradoxes, the elegant diction of Donne's sonnet, now I can no longer hear that poem without a keen sense of regret, disappointment, because I think it is fundamentally mistaken. I think Donne makes a theological mistake which St. Paul sometimes makes, which he hints at in the passage from this morning's epistle, a mistake which has come to bother me very much.

The problem is this: most all of us, at one time or another, begin to think of God as a sort of divine, loving superhero: Superman in theological white robes. Like Paul, we cry out, "Who will deliver me from this body of death?" Like Donne, we plead that God batter into our hearts, that God make up for our weakness by using God's own super-strength to *make us* better. That's a serious *mis*understanding of who God is, of how we are to live with our God.

This is a mistake which, I think, comes from something good. I think a great part of this mistake comes when we have a keen awareness of our own limitations, and at the same time we turn in love and trust and hope to our God. We turn to God offer us the strength and support which we have been promised. And all of that is very, very, good.

In St. Paul's case, we know that the limitations he bewailed were connected with his having been responsible for the persecution and (probably) the death of some of the first Christians. Paul is sensitive, we may think *overly* sensitive, about his past; he counts himself as the least among the apostles, and acknowledges to the Corinthians that he is counted among the rubbish of this world, the dregs of all things. Now we know that Paul wanted to be the most outstanding at whatever he became: the bride at every wedding, the corpse at every funeral, as we say. So we can take Paul's extravagant language here as more of a rhetorical flourish than an actual claim to have been a trash-picking apostle, the bottom-of-the-barrel saint. Still, Paul is deeply troubled by his acute awareness that something in him has rebelled against God; he cannot rest easy, because he knows that sin and death haunt his foot steps, that they threaten his spiritual integrity at every moment.

John Donne had a lot in common with Paul. No, he hadn't persecuted and killed Christians for their faith, but he had been a Roman Catholic, and in seventeenth-century Britain, that seemed almost as bad. Donne spent much of his youth as a notorious rakehell—what we might call a party animal—who repudiated the Catholic Church when he was young, and then, when he was older, when he recognized the truth of the gospel, yet held back from becoming involved with the Church of

England because he could not be sure that he was entering the church with suitable motives. The problem was that he had spent his life in various opportunistic careers; he was a politician, and military adventurer, and he flirted with various wealthy women from whom he received financial support. He reminds me a little of the roles Groucho Marx used to play: a witty, clever, self-interested politician and playboy. When Donne's heart turned to God, when he knew that he loved God dearly, he still could not shake off the lingering fear that penitence and religious life were just another fad in his quest for thrills.

I, too, have lingered in some of the byways where rowdy Jack Donne spent languorous nights of self-indulgence; I, too, have felt a deeply-rooted hesitation to commit myself to a way of life which might not hold my attention any longer than a hot new record album. I have felt the weakness of my flesh which drives Paul to pray for God to deliver him, which impels Donne to beg, "Batter my heart, overthrow me, break me, burn me, imprison me." And once again, I want to tell you that the spiritual insight which reveals the frailty of human life, which leads us to confess our need for God, these are very good.

But from this very good beginning comes a fruit which is beautiful on the outside, yet dangerously sickening inside.

For the Lord our God is *not* a white-caped superhero who flies to our rescue, and our persistent notion that God might be that way is a demonic snare. *Yes*, God is our deliverer; *yes*, God has done great things for us, and will continue working marvelous changes in our midst, despite our best efforts to keep everything the way they've always been. But God's way is not to batter us into submission, or to overwhelm us with awesome displays of power. God's way is simply to stick with us until we can no longer deny God; God's way is in those unfashionable virtues which Paul so often commends to us: patience, perseverance, constancy, peacefulness.

Have we not learned this yet? Do we not remember that the Word of God came to Elijah not in the whirlwind, nor in earthquake nor in the fire, but in the voice of the calm silence? Do we not remember that when Jesus' disciples urged him to call down fire from heaven, he chastised them? That he insisted that

Peter not use the sword to protect him in Gethsemane? No, we have not learned; Paul did not fully learn this lesson, and John Donne's poem suggests that *he* didn't learn this lesson.

This lesson is critically important, though. We may shrug and say, "But Paul was always prone to letting his rhetoric run away with him, and Donne's poem speaks so beautifully of the recalcitrant soul's longing for God; why make a big-deal sermon out of a couple of metaphors in a poem, out of a spontaneous exclamation from one letter?" I answer, "Because as we pray, as we take delight in poetry, as we cherish favorite passages from Scripture, we are forming our lives and sensibilities in harmony with the things we pray, the things that delight us, the passages that move us." And if we pray, "Batter my heart," if we delight in poetry which portrays God as a spiritual jailer, a conquering general, if we cherish a biblical text which implores God to rescue us from our own flesh, if with John Donne we imagine a God whom we call to ravish, to rape our souls to make us pure, then we will be imagining and worshipping a false God.

The God whom we love and worship does not hate our flesh; the Word *became* flesh, and dwelt among us, full of grace and truth. The God whom we trust and call upon came not as a triumphant dictator or a magical hero. Our God is no macho slugger; our God reaches out to us, patiently and gently, putting to us the important questions of our lives, and then God refuses to leave us alone. No matter how desperately we want to turn away from God, no matter how fervently we turn our backs and then demand that God meet us on our own terms, God abides with us. And when we realize that our God *is* with us, when we realize that the strength we need to get through our troubles is at hand, and most all, when we realize that God helps us not by hacking our enemies to bits, not by beating down our doubts not by raping our souls, but by loving, trusting, forgiving, and preserving us, *then* we can truly and effectively receive the gentle, constant strength God offers us.

It is a real, carnal strength. It is a hard-working, costly strength. But the mystery of God's way is that the strength we use in following the Lord comes straight from God. The energy we devote to God's work, the Spirit of God indeed will restore.

To the one who has done much for God will more be given; this discipline seems painful at the time, but later it yields the peaceful fruit of righteousness to those who have been trained by it. By greeting the gentle, patient God, by taking a godly patience, persistence, and constancy into our own lives, we will endure whatever difficulties we encounter. We will endure, and we will prevail over all the obstacles that weigh us down. We will endure, and we will prevail, and we will be delivered from our labors; but not by a conquering, battering Lord. We will be delivered by our Lord, who called, "Come to me, all you who labor and are heavy laden, and I will give you rest; for I am gentle and humble in heart, and you will find rest for your souls. For my yoke is easy, and my burden is light."

REQUIEM

Romans 8:14-19, 34-35, 37-39

In all these things we are more than conquerors through him who loved us. For I am convinced that neither death, nor life, nor angels, nor rulers, nor things present, nor things to come, nor powers, nor height, nor depth, nor anything else in all creation, will be able to separate us from the love of God in Christ Jesus our Lord.

In the Name of God: Father, Son and Holy Spirit— *Amen.*

 Last Wednesday was the feast day of St. Agnes. The church commemorated the life of a woman who bore witness faithfully throughout a short life, who was executed—burned at the stake—in the year 304 for her faith before she had a chance to become a mother. We celebrated the wisdom and perseverance of a woman whose name means, "pure" in Greek, or "lamb" in Latin; and we offered this prayer in her memory: "Almighty and everlasting God, you choose those whom the world deems powerless to put the powerful to shame: Grant us so to cherish the memory of your youthful martyr Agnes, that we may share her pure and steadfast faith in you; through Jesus Christ our Lord, who lives and reigns with you and the Holy Spirit, one God, for ever and ever."

 Last week, Caroline Agnes Hodgins was reborn to eternal life in the communion of the saints. Her life is in some ways a perfect complement to that of her ancient namesake; our sister Agnes lived a long life; she was a devoted mother, and she entered her everlasting rest in peace. As we struggle to come to terms with her sudden affliction and death, we are called to recall the lesson of the saints, the lesson which we have been taught in Christ, who overcame death and the grave, and who has offered to all the saints the possibility of sharing in his victory.

 For we share with St. Agnes the faith that Christ, having conquered death, will return again to raise us all to eternal life.

We share her trust that we will then be united with all the saints in the mystery of resurrection life. We believe that in that day, there will be no pain or sorrow, but only the joy of heavenly communion with our Lord and with the saints. We believe that nothing can separate the faithful from the love of God in Christ Jesus our Lord.

We believe these things, but we wish there were more for us to do. We wish that there were some door we could tear open, or some dangerous quest we could take, some enemy we could overcome or some challenge we could face so that we could bring that glorious reunion closer, by the sheer force of our will. We wish we could focus our grief to win that victory for ourselves. We wish that we could conquer death and the grave.

Now, we who are children of God, who are sisters and brothers of the saints who have gone before us, will feel grief and loss; we who have learned to love one another will inevitably miss one another when we are parted. We who are joined into the one body of Christ in baptism will not rest easily when one of us dies. We long to struggle, to overcome death on behalf of those whom we love.

But that is a battle that the saints have already won. Death has no hold over the saints; they are not captives of sin, because they have cleansed themselves in the saving blood of the Lamb. The saints have already won their battle with death, and as we grieve, as we long to burst the boundary that separates them from us, they stand beside us. While we can not touch or hold them, they have already found us, and they strive to console us. They encourage us with their example of patient endurance, of pride and strength. They teach us how we can be more than conquerors by resisting death not through vain struggles or anxieties, but through trust and prayer and discipleship.

This is the victory of the saints: not that we try single-handedly to defeat Death, to bring back the departed—but rather that we abide in their presence, that we take comfort in the salvation of which they partake. And inspired by their example, we will live, with joy and pride and strength, in the light of their witness. We will follow in the ways that St. Agnes of old, and our own sister Agnes today, have taught us: ways of loving-kindness, faithful service, graciousness, devotion to family and friends, and trust in the God who reaches out to us.

We are not separated from Agnes. We are not alone. We are only just awaiting the day when all the children of God are reunited *in victory* over time and death. On that day, death will be swallowed up in victory, the saints' victory and ours, which is given us by God through our Lord Jesus Christ. This afternoon—in thanksgiving for Agnes's victory over death, and in anticipation of our reunion with her—we join in a prayer, today praying not for the saint of long ago, but for the saint who is special to St. James' Church, who has touched all of our lives with her special grace and love:

Almighty and everlasting God, you choose those whom the world deems powerless to put the powerful to shame: Grant us so to cherish the memory of your devoted witness Agnes, that we may share her pure and steadfast faith in you; through Jesus Christ our Lord, who lives and reigns with you and the Holy Spirit, one God, for ever and ever.

PROPER 28

Daniel 12:1-13; Hebrews 10:31-39; Mark 13:14-23

Do not throw away your confidence, which has a great reward. For you have need for endurance, so that you may do the will of God and received what is promised. "For yet a while, and the coming one shall come and shall not delay; but my righteous one shall live by faith."

In the Name of God: Father, Son and Holy Spirit— *Amen.*

    It has been a hard year for many of us at St. James. It seems that every time I come to Tampa, I am told that someone's beloved sister, or cousin, mother or father has died; indeed, a number of the saints here at St. James have died since spring. It has been a hard year, but when we face the hard challenge that grief poses against life, we are called to remember these messages from Scripture: first, that we may trust that God has accepted those whom we love, whose loss we mourn; and second, that if we take seriously the comfort and rest which our Lord has offered, then we must also take seriously the Lord's demand that those who call on the name of Jesus live out their faith with constant discipleship. We are assured of the celestial blessings Daniel writes about, but we are also assured that God respects us, takes us seriously enough to insist that we make our lives count.

    The first point to stress is that the God who welcomes those who have died is a loving and forgiving God, a God who seeks out the weak and the sinful and promises to give them strength; a God who chooses the oppressed and outcasts, and offers them rule over all things; a God who offers eternal life to those whose deaths trouble our hearts. Our God offers salvation to all who will accept salvation—including many folks whom we church people perhaps wish God would just kick out. God goes after the lost sheep, the drunken bar-flies, the street kids and the dealers, and God brings them in—whether we like it or not. So if God has told us that people will be there from all neighborhoods, from the dirty, smelly streets as well as the sparkling subdivisions, if God has told us that hookers and pickpockets are just as likely to be there as the clergy and the judges, well, then we may be assured that our saints are among the elect to whom God promises the brightness of the stars, shining for eternal life.

Because—as I told you a couple of weeks ago, and as the lesson from Hebrews said today—though it is a fearful thing to fall into the hands of the living God, yet the helpless, the weak, the heartsick mourners are exactly the kind of people God would not desert. Those who are already weeping and anxious at their loved ones' death, God will comfort; and God will not grieve them with the possibility that their beloved has been excluded from the divine grace of heavenly life.

But there must be some people destined for what Daniel calls "everlasting contempt," for what Matthew calls "the outer darkness, where there is wailing and gnashing of teeth"; there must be some folks who may end up in that spot. The saints have taught us that it's just not true to say that we *know* God will save all people; who then won't be saved? Who is at risk?

Sisters and brothers, I think the answer to that question is: maybe it's us. That is, while we can trust that God will not abandon those who have died, those of us who are yet alive are still at risk of turning away from the God who has called us, who still calls us, who calls us in the morning when we're waking up, who calls us in the nighttime when we lie down to sleep, who calls us in our dreams and in our daily work. We're the ones who are at risk—and that's why we can never assume that everyone will be saved, or even that *we* will be saved. Jesus points out, over and over again, that the people who think highly of themselves, the people who work wonders, the people who are on the vestry or who are elected bishop, the people who trust that Jesus has already saved a special place at the head table just for them—these people are in big danger, and they run the risk of getting a nasty surprise. Jesus warns that he will say to some of them, "Get away from me; I never knew you."

The warning in lessons like today's reading from Daniel is concerned not for those whom we mourn, but for we who remain alive. Otherwise there would be no point for the warnings which the Bible constantly attaches to these texts. The point of lessons like these is to remind us that God cares enough about us to let us make our lives the way we want them—whether God wants them that way or not. God respects us. God commissions us to make our lives a beautiful offering, an image of the love and care God has shown to us; but God doesn't *make* that happen for us. Instead, God allows us to fulfill our side of the contract however we see fit. And if we think we'll be proud to offer to our God a life that's a sloppy combination of greed, pride, deception, and self-indulgence—well, then we've made a big mistake. We need to return to God a life that's been shaped by faith, polished by charity, decorated only by the cross of Christ as a symbol of our service.

Jesus told his disciples to live every minute as though it would be our last minute on earth, as though every beggar would be the last person we had a chance to help; as though every word we spoke were our last chance to speak the Word of truth and life to our neighbors; as though every moment was our last chance to offer God the sacrifice of praise and thanksgiving which we make by serving those in need. If we live this way, we never worry about when the moment actually will be. We need not chase after every new hero, every would-be Messiah; we won't be concerned if we hear rumors, or if someone comes on the TV and says he knows that God will bring it all to an end on such-and-such a date, or if our neighbor says that the break-up of the Soviet Union and the peace talks in the Mideast mean that God is coming soon. Sisters and brothers, there will always be false signs, false prophets, ready to say that *this* is the moment or *that* will be the day. Don't believe it. Instead, take care of your own calling. When God calls you, then follow. Follow in the risky path of discipleship, and the exact day and hour won't matter to you any more than they did to Jesus.

It will be difficult. No one walks that way easily. There will be hard struggles. There will be ridicule. That's part of following the cross. But don't throw out your trust in God, because that trust is itself the gift from God. That trust is what can get you through the hard times. That trust is what can redeem your sufferings. That trust, that gift of faith by which God's righteous ones live, comes to you in one package with the call to follow and the strength to walk in God's ways. The trust, the call and the strength to follow are all one in God's gift of faith to you. Don't throw out your trust in God—for you have need of endurance, so that you may do the will of God and receive what is promised.

The letter to the Hebrews quotes those words from Habakkuk: "Yet a little while and the coming one shall come and not delay; but my righteous ones shall live by faith." This faith is nothing other than trust in the God who calls us, trust in the God who gives us the strength to keep going in spite of hard times, trust in the God who has welcomed our friends among the saints, and trust that God will judge us with the mercy which is promised to those who show mercy to their neighbors. Sisters and brothers, let *us* live by that kind of faith, so that *we* may do the will of God and receive what is promised.

3 ADVENT

John 1:6-8, 19-28

They asked John, "Why then do you baptize, if you are neither the Messiah, nor Elijah, nor the prophet?"

In the Name of God Almighty,
      the Blessed Trinity on High—*Amen.*

"Why then do you baptize?" The Judean visitors wanted to know what John was up to, and this morning I'm wondering what John was up to. I suspect *we* baptize out of habit, or a sense of tradition, more than anything else. Baptism, as we know from the catechism, is the sacrament by which God adopts us into as God's children and makes us members of the Christ's Body, the Church, and inheritors of the Kingdom of God. But *why* do we baptize? And why did *John*, who had no habit or tradition of baptizing, baptize? What is baptizing, anyway?

    The short answer, church, is that baptizing is washing, cleaning. We can have a debate from now to New Year's about whether you have to *immerse* someone to really clean them, or whether you can *rinse* them with a sprinkling; but however you go about it, baptizing is about cleaning. Eventually John did so much of it that it became his nickname: John the Cleanser. And when word got back to Jerusalem that some fellow in animal-hide was down by the Jordan washing people off before the arrival of God, the Judeans sent some visitors to find out why John was cleaning.

    It seems from the story as though they had expectations about why someone would baptize, and it seems as though they thought only the Messiah, or Elijah, or someone like that would do the cleaning. John told them, "No, you just don't know what God has in store for you this time—even though he's standing right in the middle of you." John was cleaning up, washing everyone up to prepare them for the greatest of all guests, and the Pharisees were standing over by the side wondering what was going on around them.

John isn't being tricky with them, I don't think; he doesn't seem like a smart-aleck to me. After all, if anyone was going to understand about washing up, if anyone was going to understand the way God would deal with our sins, it ought to have been the Pharisees. But then. . . . But then, people who ought to know what's going on are frequently the last to get word. Frequently our mayors and governors and presidents, the people who ought to be *leading* the nation, are way behind the voters; frequently, they're years out of touch with real people's lives, with what it's like to have a hard-working job and go to the market, to lock the door at night and pray for safety. Sometimes even our priests and bishops fall out of touch with what's happening around them, and they try to turn the church toward a goal that's just *not* where it ought to be headed.

Now, when our leaders get off track that way, there's always a temptation to think they must be right, and *we* must be ignorant or short-sighted. After all, *they're* the leaders; they're the ones whom we've entrusted to guide us right. They're *experts*, they're the ones who above all other people ought to know what's best for us. Sometimes that works right; when you climb up to Capitol Hill, sometimes you can see the horizons better, sometimes you can see further down the road toward what we're coming up to. But sometimes when you get elected to the Capitol, sometimes when you're consecrated up to the Cathedral's towers, it gets a little cloudy at the top and you can't see what's happening down in the streets. Sometimes the leaders are so far out ahead, they get lost; sometimes the experts are *so* expert that they need regular folks to take them by the hand and show them what's going on.

So when the Pharisees heard that there was some unauthorized theological activity going on down by the Jordan River, they sent their advance men to figure it out. "Why do you baptize," they asked John. "What's going on here?" John tried to give them a clue: "I'm just doing the job God called me to: I'm the voice of one crying out in the wilderness, Make straight the way of the Lord." (They didn't get it.) John tried again: "I'm washing them down with water; but there's someone standing right there among you whose shoes I'm not worthy to untie." The next day he's going to point right to Jesus and say, "Look, there he is, the Lamb of God," and the Pharisees *still* aren't going to get it. They'll still be standing there asking, "Why all this *washing*, though, John?"

Before we smile at the Pharisees, before we fuss at our misguided leaders, we need to pay close attention to John. John wasn't waiting around for the Pharisees to catch his drift. John wasn't complaining that no one understood that it was time for baptizing. John wasn't waiting for permission from the Sanhedrin—he went down to the Jordan and *baptized,* cause he knew the time was close at hand and we'd better *wash* that sin out of our lives, because he knew we'd better *clean up* our wedding garments, because the feast is coming and we want to be found in our very *best* of clothes. John took matters into his own hands.

Sisters and brothers, we've got such a *big* church and a *big* government, it's easy to get into the habit of calling the Pharisees and saying, "We've got a problem here—you come down and figure it out for us." This morning, though, John stands up in bright sunlight of the Jordan dawn and gets to work, cleaning and scrubbing and preparing the way of the Lord. This morning, God's way is pushing and struggling and pressing into the world, like a baby pushing to be born. The God who is about to create a new heavens and a new earth, the God who is set to rejoice in Jerusalem, who will adopt us all as children, our God is pressing on us like labor pains coming on a woman who's ready to bring that child into the world. She's not going to wait for permission from the president—she's not going to wait to be blessed by a bishop. She's going ahead to do what she has to do, like Isaiah prophesying the peaceable kingdom, like Paul preaching the gospel in season and out of season, like John cleaning up a people fit for the coming of the Lord. When the time comes, she's going to do what she has to do—and the Pharisees will just have to figure it out as best they can.

"Why are you baptizing?" Because that's the *least* we can do, the first thing we can do to get ready. Those labor pains are getting closer together, says John, those pains are coming closer together and we have to make room for a baby. If the leaders won't make a place in the capitol, then we'll clean out a manger. But soon, and *very* soon, there's going to be a baby born among us, and we want to be a ready people. So we're setting about cleaning up our lives, cleaning up our parish, scrubbing away at old sins and chasing away the temptations to start new ones—rejoicing, praying, giving thanks, holding fast to what is good.

Sisters and brothers, no one can stop that baby. No politician, no priest, can stop that baby being born. The baby is what's important—not the Pharisees. You don't bow down before the Pharisees, you don't know their names; you aren't going to stop the Lord's work. It's not the time for that. Keep an eye on what's happening, watch out for that baby, and make a place in your lives where that baby is safe, where people don't hurt or destroy, where we're with John, baptizing, cleaning up, preparing God's way, because unlike the Pharisees, *we know who we're looking for*. Let them put on puzzled expressions and ask, "Why are you baptizing?" *You* stand with John; keep washing and cleaning, and the God of peace will indeed sanctify you entirely, and keep your spirit and soul and body sound at the coming of that baby, of our Lord Jesus Christ.

PROPER 15

Proverbs 9:1-6; Ephesians 5:15-20; John 6:53-59

Lay aside immaturity and live, and walk in the way of insight.

In the Name of God Almighty, the Blessed Trinity— *Amen.*

    I have to talk to our Newcomers Committee, to Galen and Doug about this: a new approach to evangelism, from the Book of Proverbs! "Hey, you that are simple, come on in here! You senseless people, come, eat and drink!" We hadn't thought about making a special appeal to the simple-minded, immature citizens of Evanston—but it just might work. Here we have a scriptural model that specifies this method for building up our congregation and spreading the good news of the Way of Jesus Christ. Here we had been working on our program, our communications, our presence in the community, when the secret of attracting our neighbors to worship beside may simply lie in hollering, "Hey, you fools—you have no life in you! Come here and we'll tell you what's what!"

    At St. Luke's, of course, we're much too polite to talk that way. Indeed, just in general, that's not our angle on evangelism. We can imagine too clearly how we would feel, how we *do* feel when others assure us that *they* have all the answers and *we* need to sit still and listen to *them*. From where we stand, Wisdom has nothing whatever to do with calling people ninnies or fools. If folks were scandalized when Jesus called them to think twice about the shape of their faith, how much more reason do they have to be troubled if we come around calling them names as a strategy for recruiting them into the church.

    Wisdom teaches *us* that few people think of themselves as fools, no matter how obvious it looks to anyone else. One of the marks of the greatest fools is their incapacity to recognize their folly, a characteristic that we see spotlighted in flashing neon in many academic and, all too often, in religious circles. Wisdom teaches us that we won't persuade one of these expert fools—or anyone—by insulting them. Even a self-aware, humble fool will probably draw back if we call him senseless when we invite him to join us. The emphasis in our evangelism falls not on explaining how misguided everyone *else* might be. Our invitation highlights the *goodness* we taste in the holy food and drink with which Jesus feeds us, and our evangelism extols the *joy* of singing psalms and hymns and spiritual songs among ourselves, singing and making melody to the Lord in our hearts. In our joy, we long to swing open our doors and welcome more and more of our neighbors; as Jesus welcomes and feeds us, we would welcome and share this food of life with our neighbors.

That's *true* hospitality, dear friends. Such hospitality, at its deepest, arises in our hearts as a longing to offer all the goodness that we enjoy to everyone around. Evangelism is another way of describing a generosity that *will not* withhold from others the good things that God has given to *us*. We have no other excuse for evangelizing—not that we like having a full church, or that we're trying to build the budget back up, or that if we have to wake up Sunday morning, our neighbors can jolly well get up and go to church too.

We have no other excuse for evangelizing, but for just the same reason, we have no choice but to evangelize. We are obliged to make known this astonishing generosity, to proclaim the love of God that overflows to wash us from the sins that cling to us so stickily, the love that overflows to refresh and cool us from the heat of daily toil, the love that sweeps us along in the gentle current of God's Way of peace and patience to join one another in a communion the draws all people together to the everlasting feast in the house of Wisdom. So spectacular a prospect can't be hid under a bushel, stuffed away in a closet, but we must cooperate with God to make the our faith perceptible, even visible, even tangible. It's faith *alive,* growing, faith *in action*.

Faith *belongs* to action, because, on the whole, the brain is a highly overrated organ for believing. I believe much more immediately with my feet (for instance) than with my brain. Or with my knees, that bend in confession because they understand, more firmly than my brain does, that I have not walked steadily in God's ways. Or I believe with my hands, when I reach for a dollar bill for the woman who's selling *Streetwise* in front of Jewel-Osco; or I believe with my ears, when my friends here or at Seabury pour out their stories of hard times and challenges, of joys and relief. My arms believe, as they embrace another to join in the peace of God, or to share communion. My eyes believe, when I can look in *your* eyes and greet you as my sister in Christ, my brother in Christ. We worship this sensuous way, sisters and brothers, because the knees that bend and the hands that make the sign of the cross and the noses that smell incense and the throats that sing with joy are all part of our believing, and sometimes they're the most profound part of our faith. My brain believes, all right, but my body leads the way, and in the end my body preaches the truth about the gospel I believe, by showing anyone, everyone, how I live.

That's a weakness with brands of evangelizing that focus on debating with skeptics, establishing the irrefutable truth of doctrinal claims. This kind of evangelism treats brain-believing as though *it* were primary. These modes of reaching out tacitly identify our neighbors as fools, as simple-minded people who need instruction from us in the way things really work. This kind of evangelism lends itself to rhetoric about our *winning* souls for Christ, about *our* having the responsibility for bringing about the salvation of souls—where the Wisdom of Jesus and the saints has always taught us quite the opposite: that our proofs and our assent to propositions are frail, fond things, while *God* and *God alone* is in the saving business. The truth that we stake our lives on shines from our actions, in the same way that we show our faith in gravity by not jumping off towers; when we put our faith into gear, when we follow the disciples' way of giving, of healing, of trusting, of enduring, of loving one another, we let that hope shine.

Our hope radiates through our lives more than just our words, because everyone has a line, everyone has a rap, a shtick, and everyone believes *something* or other. We don't have anything special to offer the world by way of *talk*; we just sat through four political conventions, Democrats, Republicans, Reform Party, and Greens, and right now we're acutely aware that there is not a shortage of talk. We have something different to offer, something that won't put you to sleep but will raise you to life. We have something different to share, and if we hoard it, if we squirrel it away, if we stockpile it for ourselves, we lose it. The good news is not ours to keep, but we grow in maturity, in depth of spirit, by walking in the Way of insight, by embodying our Way of patience and gentleness and sharing in a world that thinks—if our mass culture provides any indication—a world that thinks most Christians are uptight prudes or obnoxious hypocrites, that church is a waste of time, that the wisdom of the saints amounts to an arbitrary heap of nonsensical laws, that most clergy are secret drunks or sexual predators. *Talking* gospel only confirms what our neighbors think about us; it's words and rules, and who needs it?

We have a chance, though, to surprise the world. We have a chance to be *exceptions* to what we're expected to be, we have the chance not to in*sult* our neighbors, but to in*vite* them, to show the sisters and brothers among whom we work and walk and drive and shop that Wisdom has built the house, Wisdom has set the table and prepared the meal; around here, the only fool is the one who won't stop talking and come to eat. The waters of faith are not bottled up for the effete connoisseurs of theological nuance, but they constitute us, they make us what we are, creatures of water, *holy* water, and we're here to work, to walk in the way of insight.

1 CHRISTMAS

Isaiah 61:10-62:3; Galatians 3:23-25, 4:4-7; John 1:1-18

He was in the world, and the world was made through him, yet the world knew him not. He came to his own home, and his own people received him not. But to those who received him, who believed in his name, he gave power to become children of God.

In the Name of the Father, and of the Son,
    and of the Holy Spirit— *Amen.*

    I used to work in a nursing home in Connecticut, and there we had a weekly Bible study. I remember that at one session—I don't recall what text we were discussing—one of the ladies was claiming loudly and insistently that when Christ came again, *she* would recognize him. Other members of the group tried to suggest that she take a more humble attitude; maybe she *hoped* hard that she'd recognize him, or that she figured she'd *probably* recognize him. But she stuck with her claim. No two ways about it; she knew Jesus, and she'd recognize her savior when he came.
    Well, maybe she's right. But if the pictures in her room were the ground for her certainty that she'd recognize Jesus, I have to doubt that she was right. The Jesus she saw every day, and the Jesus *I* knew for the first fifteen or so years of my life, was about 6 foot tall; he had light brown hair, mostly straight, but with a little wave in it; had skin about my color, only perfectly smooth and creamy; blue eyes, of course. It was kind of hard to imagine that Jesus being tough enough to make much of a fuss when he drove the moneychangers out of the temple. With a picture of Jesus like that, we wouldn't have recognized Jesus when he came the *first* time. And I doubt very much that Jesus will look like that the next time.
    Even the people who were expecting God's Messiah, the anointed one of Israel, didn't recognize Jesus. Now, there probably wasn't a real fever pitch of excitement about *the*

Messiah coming at Jesus' time; after all, there had been a number of Messiahs running around Palestine over the past few years, and there would be a few more after Jesus. Messiahs—"Anointed Ones"—were a dime a dozen in Jesus' time, and though they worked up a lot of excitement for a while, they usually came to a bad end. There was Simon, who'd been a servant of Herod the Great, Simon bar Giora, Athronges the Judean shepherd, Judas the son of the terrorist Ezekias, and Judas's own son Menahem, himself a terrorist; and Simon bar Kochba, "the son of the star." Among this crowd of Messiahs—some of whom gathered armies large enough to fight off the Roman army, at least for a little while—this pacifist from Nazareth was so little known that it wasn't until his story reached the very people who *hadn't* been expecting him that more than a handful of followers believed in his name. "He was in the world, and the world was made through him, yet the world knew him not. He came to his own home, and his own country received him not."

When we think about recognizing the returning Christ, we have to remember that *this* time, *we* are the ones in his own home; *we* are the ones at risk of not recognizing him. That's why there is the theme, constantly repeated through the New Testament (and especially in our Advent lessons), that we should watch out. That's why we're told over and over that we *won't* know when he's coming, and that we oughtn't to listen to people who will tell us "There he is!" "Here he is!" When Jesus says, "The first shall be last, and the last shall be first," or "Those who humble themselves will be exalted, but those who exalt themselves will be humbled"—that's talking about *us*. Try to imagine for a minute some way in which we—sitting pretty here this morning—could possibly think of ourselves as "the humble ones." But if *we're* so far from being the humble ones of the earth—and even the humblest American has a big job thinking he's anywhere *near* as low down as most other folks in the world—if we are so far from being the last, how sure can we be that we will recognize the Lord who was not recognized by the good religious people to whom he came once before?

Jesus tells us that there is one way we can be sure to recognize him: it is by clothing the needy, feeding the hungry, by receiving the little ones in his name. We won't know when he has been with us; in the parable of the sheep and the goats, the sheep whom Jesus gathers to himself are *surprised* that they have fed him, clothed him, given him a drink. But the point isn't that we should have a mental mug shot of Jesus so we can look out for his picture on the news (I saw a tabloid in the supermarket the other day saying that the face of Jesus was appearing in the sky over North America, but a year or two ago Jesus' face was appearing on a tortilla shell, and before that it was on someone's freezer). The point is that when Jesus comes again, he—or *she!*—will not be so different from the Jesus we know, the Jesus who called us to serve God by serving the lowest of the low, by suffering the evils that come along with devotion to God rather than cashing in on self-interest. There won't be a penalty for not recognizing Jesus' facial features, but there will be a severe cost for not recognizing the opportunity he has given us to become God's children by serving those in need, those who—like Mary and Joseph in Bethlehem—don't have a place to rest their heads. And before we start rushing to note that these teachings are, after all, metaphorical exaggerations, rhetorical flourishes, we should listen to the passages where Jesus explicitly reminds us that his friends are the ones who hear what he says, and *do it*. No excuses, no parables or puzzles; *just do it.*

When we start feeling superior to the Judaeans to whom Jesus came, who knew him not, who received him not, we need to remember that there are plenty of nice, polite, church-going people who do not recognize Jesus when he comes to them today, just as there were plenty of Jesus' own people who didn't recognize him before. I'm sure some of those people are like my friend at the nursing home, certain that they know just what they're expecting. But Jesus has given us a bigger job than simply waiting around for his return visit, and if we live up to that job we won't have anything to worry about. At the time he returns, it it will not be a chorus of gentlemen in tuxes and ladies in designer gowns who sing to welcome him, but the snips and scraps of humanity will form the holy choir which will sing out the words of our reading from the book of Isaiah:

Let me rejoice in the Lord with all my heart,
let me exult in my God;
for he has robed me in deliverance,
and arrayed me in victory,
like a bridegroom with his garland,
or a bride decked in her jewels
As the earth puts forth her blossom
or plants in the garden burst into flower,
so will the Lord God make his victory and renown
blossom before all nations.
For Zion's sake I shall not keep silent,
for Jerusalem's sake I shall not be quiet,
until her victory shines forth like the sunrise,
her deliverance like a blazing torch,
and the nations see your victory
and all the kings your glory.
Then you will called by a new name
which the Lord himself will announce;
you will be a glorious crown in the Lord's hand,
a royal diadem held by your God.

Jesus has called us to open our homes to him, to make him welcome in our lives by welcoming his ambassadors—that is, his *apostles*, the ones he has sent to us—the homeless, the hungry and thirsty, the naked, the prisoners, the little ones who don't count for anything in the world.

And to those who receive him, who believe in his name, he will give power to become children of God.

HOLY NAME

Exodus 34:1-8; Romans 1:1-7; Luke 2:15-21

After eight days had passed, it was time to circumcise the child; and he was called Jesus, the name given by the angel before he was conceived in the womb.

In the Holy Name of God,
           made known to us in Christ Jesus— *Amen.*

It comes as a surprise to many people that Jesus was Jewish. It comes as even more of a surprise when they learn that, according to the gospels, he was an observant Jew; he was circumcised and bar mitzvahed, he was observed the Jewish festivals, he taught that the Law of Moses would never pass away until heaven and earth pass away at the consummation of all things.

Our Lord Jesus Christ was a thoroughly Jewish man. He observed the Law; he went to the festivals; when he healed lepers, he sent them to the priests in accordance with the rules in the book of Leviticus; he paid the tax which supported the Temple in Jerusalem; he went to synagogue services regularly; he even taught people to do what the Pharisees said. Jesus was Jewish not only in a remote, abstract, spiritual way, but he was Jewish in all the very concrete and particular ways of everyday life. He not only lived by the laws of Moses as they are written in Scripture, but he also commended the Pharisaic interpretation of those laws, and in his teachings he reproduced many sayings which were be at home in the tradition of the rabbis.

What is more, even though the next generations of Christians gradually recognized that the Law of Moses was not binding on those who came before God in Christ, yet the Law itself was held up as a sign of God's good providence for Israel; God taught Israel the way of Life, and gave Israel the Law as the mark of the covenant which would forever bind God and this chosen people. St. Paul taught that the Law was holy, good, and just, that although God had revealed a new righteousness apart from the Law in Christ Jesus, yet the Law was not bad, nor are those who obey the Law misguided.

So both in the life and teachings of our Lord and in the lives and teachings of the apostles, we find compelling examples of practicing one's faith not only with good deeds, with moral behavior, but at the same time with practicing the customs and expectations of one's community. Both Jesus and the apostles teach us that part of Christian life involves regularly taking part in the services and activities of the church.

That may seem unreasonable. It may seem silly to suggest that our attendance at church, our observance of special feast days, even our making the sign of the cross or bowing at the name of Jesus, make some kind of difference to our spiritual well-being. But let me suggest some good reasons for thinking that these practices are quite important indeed. Not only do we have the example of Jesus and his immediate followers; we have the evidence of our own lives.

We know that practice, that the habit of working on a particular skill or capacity day in and day out, inevitably makes us better at what we are doing. The more I type, the more I practice the *right* way to type, the faster and more accurate I get. The more I work on my Greek grammar, the better I can read and translate. The more I cook, the better I can gauge just how much longer a particular dish needs to stay in the oven. While there may be some people who are blessed with the capacity to be great at something without practice, those people are rare indeed; they certainly aren't *me*. Instead, the lesson which we have to admit is that practice, habit, make things into a vital part of our lives; practice makes us better at whatever we try.

The opposite is true as well. They say you never forget how to ride a bicycle, but when I got a bicycle a while back, after not having ridden a bike for almost fifteen years, I was a much worse bicycle rider than I am today. If I were to pick up a guitar—and we all may be thankful that I can't reach one—I would play it as badly as someone who has never played, because it has been so long since I even tried. The same goes with our life of worship. As we leave off going to church today, as we sleep late another day, as we omit our daily prayers in a hurry one morning, then forget them the next, we are gradually becoming weaker and less regular worshippers. We are losing our facility for worshipping God; we are losing our touch, our sense for just how we ought to live our lives.

Now, not only is church-y behavior important as practice for worship; it's also important as a way of training our bodies, of forming our muscles and organs and reflexes, to the new identity we develop as followers of Jesus. It's easy enough to say, "Oh, well, I believe and everything, but I don't have to go to church, and I don't hold with making crosses or kneeling." But it's just these exercises which help train us to react to life not only as thinking *heads*, but as people whose *bodies* are trained for holy living as well. If we train ourselves with these gestures, these habits, it is these gestures and habits that will come to us if we find ourselves in a crisis; and if we remember to make the sign of a cross, we are more likely to remember to pray to the crucified Lord. We are more likely to remember that we live in the hands of a God who cares for us. And we may hope that hands that are trained for making the sign of the cross might hesitate before they pick up a hypodermic needle or an automatic pistol.

We are called to assent to God, to worship God, not only with our minds, but with our bodies as well. That's why the people of Israel practice circumcision; that's why the apostles kept the Law, even though they were—in Christ—freed from the Law; that's why we, too, train our bodies, form our habits in holy ways. Sure, there's no *need* to go to church for every service, just as there's no *need* for Wayne Gretzky to practice puck-handling, for Michael Jordan to practice shooting baskets. The point is, if we want to stay in practice, if we don't want our faith to get flabby, if we don't want to lose our sense of what's fitting and right (and what *isn't*), then we have to keep *practicing* our faith, not just in doing good deeds, but in the routine exercises of going to church—even the times we don't want to, even on New Year's Day when the preacher is some boring professor who doesn't know our neighborhood, maybe even who doesn't understand us or our lives. We need these theological exercises to keep our bodies and minds trained on God. We have to keep practicing our faith in order to keep *spiritually* fit, so that when our Lord comes to us and calls us, we will be found well-prepared.

PROPER 12

1 Kings 3:5-12; Romans 8:26-30; Matthew 13:31-33, 44-49a

The kingdom of heaven is like treasure hidden in the field, which someone found and hid; then in his joy he goes and sells all that he has and buys that field.

May only God's Word be spoken,
    and may only God's Word be heard— *Amen*

Every now and then, after I have unburdened my heart on one topic or another, someone comes up and says, "Professor Adam, you have a right to your opinion about the Gulf War (or whatever other topic I've been lecturing about), but you shouldn't mix up your religion and your politics."

I do not respond well to that bit of advice; my faith and my politics are the same thing. I put no governor before God, nor any state before the communion of the saints. Any political judgments I make grow out of my understanding of the good news of our redemption and unity in our only Lord Jesus Christ.

The attitude that we ought to make a distinction between our private, internal faith and our public, external political life is one of the consequences of a sort of thinking that has gotten us into a variety of awkward messes. This way of thinking about the world decrees that some people know everything important on a topic, and they are called "experts"; other people don't count, and they are called "non-experts," or, sometimes, "lay people." I am an expert on biblical studies and postmodern critical theory; I am a non-expert on constitutional law and physical anthropology. If I say something about biblical interpretation, people have to pay attention to my statement; if I say something about physical anthropology, no one has to pay any attention to me. There are a bunch of problems with this habit of dividing up the world into experts and non-experts; the one that looks biggest to me is that this habit inclines people to think that if they want to read the Bible, they need an expert's help to understand it.

That's just nonsense. Some of the best, wisest, truest biblical interpreters have been non-experts, and I urge you never to worry too much about what biblical experts have to say. (Except for *me*, of course.)

Another bad consequence of this way of thinking is the notion that our knowledge belongs to little clubs: the biblical interpreters' club, the physical anthropologists' club, the radiology club, and so on. But if knowledge about things is broken up into little knowledge clubs, then if I come into the club that worries about how people in the United States ought to live, people expect me to talk the official public language of our government; my knowledge from the Christian theology club over here doesn't cross the border. I'm like a tourist trying to get directions at a Seven-Eleven—I speak a different language, and everyone in line wishes I'd either learn English or just go away. We don't fit into the conversations everyone else wants to have. As I said at the beginning, people tell me, "You shouldn't mix your religion into politics."

Now, I have a big complaint about that way of reasoning. For one thing, if I'm not allowed to talk about my faith in public, I don't have a whole lot more to talk about. But more than that, the assumption that people of faith should check their convictions at the door when they enter the arena of politics depends on a very flat understanding of what it means to be a human being. It depends on the notion that people are nothing more than paper dolls who dress up in different sets of convictions depending on where they're going; at church, they're Christians. In the voting booth, they're public citizens. In their offices and businesses, they're shrewd merchants who extract every ounce of profit they can from a transaction. At home, they can relax and finally be themselves by avoiding talk about any of the other roles they play: "Don't talk shop," or "Let's keep politics and religion out of this." Remarks like these show that someone has a fragmented, superficial understanding of who we are and who we are called to be, and I want none of it.

One of the crucial aspects of the Christian message is that there are to *be* no "experts" in this house of God. Or to put it the other way around, we are *all* called to be *full-time* experts on discipleship. Jesus talked about this all the time. He insisted that the disciples who wanted to be greatest could only become great by *avoiding* greatness. He taught the disciples strictly not to call any religious authorities "Father," because God is the only authority figure for followers of Jesus. He thanked God for *hiding* the most important things from experts, and for revealing the most important things to children. Why is it wrong to have experts in church? Precisely because here, *everybody* is called to be an expert; everybody is called to exercise the gift of judgment, of discernment, so that we can work together to figure out what's right and what's wrong. When we start making clergy or church wardens or vestries the *experts* on what we ought to be doing, we are falling into the terrible habit of dividing up the duty to exercise responsible judgment, the duty we all share.

This point is critically important because God claims every sphere of or lives. God doesn't just want our attention for an hour or so Sunday morning. God wants our attention Monday afternoon during the sales meeting, and on election day when we vote, and on our day off, when we're just relaxing. That, I think, is the point of two of the parables that we heard this morning. Our relation to the kingdom of heaven, to God's way of living, should be like the passer-by who found buried treasure, or the jeweler who found the magnificent pearl.

Most of the time, we are taught that these parables are about the importance of setting aside lesser things to obtain the incomparable blessings of the kingdom of heaven; we're supposed to notice the contrast between earthly goods and heavenly treasures, just as the parable of the mustard seed contrasts the small beginnings of the gospel with its great destination, and the parable of the leaven contrasts the little bit of yeast with the three bushels of flour that it leavens. The wanderer discovers a precious treasure, and by rapid decisive actions he cleverly buys the field with the treasure hidden in it. Or the merchant discovers the tremendous pearl and cashes in on the golden opportunity to buy it. But at least this morning, I want you to think of the parables of the buried treasure and the pearl of great price in a different way.

I suggest that these two parables are not so much about the difference between earthly and heavenly values so much as they are about our capacity for concentration. After all, neither parable says anything about these characters making a profit on their deals; these men traded their goods not to make a high mark-up on resale, like some first century corporate raiders. Instead, they both stress that the men in these stories give up everything simply out of their concentration on the one thing they seek. The passer-by wants the treasure more than anything else; the jeweler sells off his whole inventory just so he can have the one great pearl. The point of these parables is that we should have the wisdom to seek the *one* goal of our whole lives. The wisdom from God consists in this focused commitment to God's way.

Look at the example of Solomon. In our lection this morning, he prays for one thing only: for the wisdom properly to serve God's people as their king. Solomon certainly got a reputation for wisdom, but if we look at his career, it's not clear just how wise he was; even as the Bible repeats that there was never anyone as wise as Solomon, it tells us about some of his questionable decisions. Despite God's explicit instructions, Solomon married about a thousand women, and (though the Bible—typically—blames *them* for diverting *him*) he must not have been very wise to do that. He drafted the people of Israel to do forced labor on his vast building projects; he taxed the living daylights out of the people; he rejected the God of Israel, and started messing around with foreign gods. Solomon got off to a good start, but in the course of his reign he did just the opposite of the characters in these parables: he traded in his focus on godliness for a bushel of distractions. While he started out asking for the will only to follow in God's way, he eventually started paying more attention to the perks of his office, to his monumental infrastructure plan, to his territorial wars, to his (*ahem!*) foreign affairs. Solomon the wise became Solomon the preoccupied, the distracted; he lost track of his one calling, and he became the rotten kind of king that God had warned Israel about in 1 Samuel.

This morning's parables point in the opposite direction. They suggest that we are called to lives of *integrity*, of honest, open, direct dealing with people. But we can't attain that kind of integrity if we divide up our lives into separate little segments, each with its own set of responsibilities, each with its own goals, each with its own language and its own assumptions about what's right and wrong. The impetus to parcel out our responsibilities, to separate work from devotion from politics and from play gives us the illusion that all these fields are separate from our calling as children of heaven. There are no divisions which cut off faith from politics, or the workplace, or from our relaxation time. There are no experts who can take on the responsibility to live faithfully for you. Instead, each of us, all of us together, join to help one another put away the distractions, the divisions, the fragmentations of modern life, and come together into a life with one goal, confessing one faith, sharing one cup and one plate, in the name of our one Lord and Saviour Jesus Christ.

7 EASTER

Exodus 28:1-4, 9-10, 29-30; Acts 1:15-26; John 17:11b-19

They prayed and said, "Lord, who knowest the hearts of all men, show which one of these two thou hast chosen to take the place in this ministry and apostolate from which Judas turned aside, to go to his own place." And they cast lots for them, and the lot fell on Matthias; and he was enrolled with the eleven apostles.

In the Name of God, Father Son and Holy Spirit— *Amen.*

 There is surely some message in this lesson for a parish search committee. I wouldn't suggest that the message is that you ought to choose St. James' new vicar by rolling dice, or picking a name out of a hat, or looking for someone named Matthias. I doubt there are any candidates available who have been with you during all the time that Jesus had been among you. But it remains true that there may be something for the people of St. James' parish to carry away from this lesson in how the apostles handled their first search committee.
 First of all, you will notice that there was no paperwork. You can tell the church hadn't been going too long, because if it were more than just a few days old, there would have been an ocean of forms for Peter and the rest to fill out. Second, you will notice that they accomplished the whole search—from deciding on their profile to finding a list of candidates to nominating two finalists all the way to making their choice—in the space of just eleven verses. I don't think the search committee even met more than that one time; they were probably done in one afternoon. As we've already noticed, they chose their candidate by having a lottery. And no one is reported to have left the church because of the choice they made, although poor Joseph Barsabbas was probably fairly sad about things. Finally—and this goes beyond today's reading, so you might not realize this—this is the only time Matthias gets mentioned in the Scriptures. As soon as he

gets his job as an apostle, he vanishes into the background. Everything in the story of the early church goes on as if he weren't even there.

I mention these things not because I think you shouldn't do paperwork, or that it's better to conduct your whole search in one afternoon, or that you should make your choice at random, or that no one will be dissatisfied with your choice, or that it doesn't really make any difference who you choose. But behind these unusual characteristics of the apostolic job search we can see some notions we might keep in mind for our own parish's search.

The apostles, for instance, had a clear checklist of what the new apostle ought to have going for him. They wanted someone with experience: an apostle who had accompanied them during all the time that the Lord Jesus went in and out among them, beginning from the baptism of John until the day he was taken up from them (Ascension Day, which was last Thursday). By the same token, they wanted a candidate who knew what this Jesus movement was about: someone who had not fallen away during the hard times, someone who really understood the point of following Jesus. Their two criteria were that the new apostle had to be a faithful servant, and that he had to know what he was preaching. These were the characteristics they thought most important for a church leader.

Peter's words also show that the apostles had a clear vision of their recruit's responsibility. They wanted him to go forth as a witness of the resurrection, just as they did. That's part of what "apostle" means, after all; an apostle is an ambassador from the Risen Lord to countries where God is a stranger, an alien. From the way Peter says this, it suggests that he's not repeating that these gentlemen had to be eyewitnesses to the empty tomb; he's saying that in their *new* responsibilities, they will be witnesses to the resurrection.

They found two candidates who would do the job equally well. There was no handy way of choosing between them; either one would suit the congregation equally well. So they prayed about it, and made their choice, and that's the end of the story.

One of the most striking features of this whole story is that all the things Peter and the other apostles were looking for in a replacement for Judas were qualities which we, all of us, ought to aim for ourselves. While church leadership is a special ministry, and while being one of the twelve apostles was obviously a *very* special ministry, there was no search for a specialist. And the fact that we never hear of Matthias again in the New Testament points out that he wasn't a theological star (like Peter or Paul or our own James). What the first search committee was looking for was someone who was just a good Christian.

That's what Jesus wishes for all of us in the prayer of which we read a part for today's gospel lesson. Jesus prays that *all* of us should be witnesses to the resurrection, that we *all* would teach the world what he has taught us. He prays that we stay together in a common effort, in a church whose unity and love shows the world the kind of unity and love which come from walking closely with God. He prays that we would be the kind of disciples who show their faith in Jesus and God by doing the kind of works Jesus taught us to do. These prayers aren't just for apostles—or, more to the point, "apostleship" isn't reserved only for twelve individuals who died thousands of years ago. We are *all* called to be apostles, ambassadors, witnesses to the resurrection. Just as God sent Jesus, so Jesus sends *us* all out into the world, consecrated in his truth.

And in our search here at St. James, I suggest that you keep that point in mind. Not that you oughtn't look for someone with particular characteristics—the apostles had certain characteristics in mind. Not that you shouldn't envision a particular kind of responsibility you want for your new vicar. Not that you shouldn't go through the paperwork and time-consuming step-by-step analysis that is our modern way of flipping a coin between Matthias and Barsabbas. But instead, I suggest that at every step you bear in mind that you're not looking for someone whose identity is that of a specialist—even if that specialty seems just exactly right for this congregation. You're looking for someone whose example of Christian discipleship will help you live according to the way in which Jesus calls us. You're looking for someone who has been walking by

Jesus' side, someone who's been listening closely to the Lord. You're looking for someone who, if they weren't the person you were paying to be your vicar, would be helping out unselfishly, building up the congregation with their love and patience, bearing witness to the resurrection of the Lord. That kind of ordained minister is harder to find than we all would hope. But if you can find one or two of them to consider for this ministry, then all the paperwork, and all the time it will take to complete the search, and the difficulties that will come as some brothers and sisters are uncomfortable with the way the search is going, all these trials will work out for the best. If you find a successor to Matthias in this apostolic ministry, then you all may find yourselves looking more like apostles, too.

4 ADVENT

2 Samuel 7:4, 8-16; Romans 16:25-27; Luke 1:26-38

Mary said, "Here am I, the servant of the Lord; let it be with me according to your word."

In the Name of God Almighty,
                the Blessed Trinity on High—*Amen.*

Sometimes time just slows right down to the point of stopping. Sometimes life is rushing past us so furiously that it's all we can do to catch our breath and then, suddenly, we see events with a clarity and precision that you usually see only on the special slow-motion replays of ball games or Olympic sports—or, I have to admit, in suspense movies where a time bomb ticks down thirty seconds, but the movie uses three minutes to keep us on the edge of our seats. At a moment of crisis, at a moment when everything hangs in the balance, time just slows right down to the freezing point—and for moments that can last for hours, we wait.

That's how it is now, sisters and brothers. You know that's how it's getting to be with the children, only three days left to Christmas—time's moving *really* slowly for them. By the time Christmas Eve comes around, they'll be thinking that every clock in the house is wrong, that it *must* be morning by now, that it'll be all right to get up and look around for just a minute or two. The children know that time is passing too slowly, and when the children think that time is passing too slowly, they have a way of sharing that feeling with the rest of us.

That's how it is sometimes with politics, too. That's how it can be when you see the handwriting on the wall, when you *know* a change is going to come, but you have to sit out the agonizingly slow business of seeing that change work its way through the whole slow-moving system. That's how it can be on the job, when you know that they're downsizing and you don't want to look into the envelope that someone left on your desk this morning. That's how it can be when you're in love, when you've got it *bad*, and you want to tell someone special how you feel about them. You try to make your mouth say the words you were planning, but you stammer and hesitate and the few seconds it would take to ask a simple question—"Will you see me tomorrow night?" "Would you marry me?"—those seconds take ages to get out of your mouth, and the answers take *forever* to come back to you.

In this morning's reading, time stands still for a frightened young woman and for a messenger from God. By this point in the story, God's been working with people for ages of ages. God was working with us in the garden, but we didn't get that one right. God was working with us after the garden, but we just *would* keep sinning, and God worked a fresh start with Noah and his family. Even then we let God down another time, so God tried again through Abraham and Sarah. And this time, finally this time, the plan started to come together.

On a lonely night in the middle of a desert somewhere, God and Abraham made an agreement that we children of Abraham would keep faith with the one God of heaven and earth, that we would stick with our God through thick and thin, and God promised to stick with us. Not everyone could keep that promise all the time. There have been problems with that agreement ever since. But that's the plan God has been working with from that day, we're the *people* God has been working with. First God added the Law, to help us understand what it means to be true to God; then God gave us leaders, one after another, to remind us to shape up and fly right. And when we demanded that God give us a king—not because God thought it was best for us, but because we wouldn't stop whining and fussing like the last child to not have a Tickle-Me Elmo toy—God gave us a king. Now David wasn't the finest specimen of kingship in history. He was a poor father, an unreliable husband, a murderous rival in love. But Scripture tells us that he was totally committed to the God who had raised him up from the sheep fields, who had stayed with him through fierce battles and foolish sins, so God promised an eternal kingship in David's name. We let God down in that department too, we suffered exile and slavery, we ate the bread of adversity and the water of affliction; we ate ashes like bread, and mingled tears with our drink.

Then, in our very sorry state, when one bad thing had followed another, the Assyrians and the Babylonians and the Persians and Egyptians and the Syrians and now the Romans, now the clocks start moving more slowly. The camera closes in on a young woman, not yet married, in a village in Galilee. Kings are feasting, armies are marching, terrorists are plotting, farmers are out in the fields, but our gospel reading draws us from the great events of world politics to a woman sitting all on her own. And as she sits there, she recognizes a messenger from God, who hails her, "Greetings, favored one! The Lord is with you."

Now things are slowing down fiercely. Now you can hear a pin drop, now you can feel the world's heartbeat, now the crickets and the birds and even the angels in heaven fall silent, and Mary just sits and wonders. So the angel lays out the plan. "Do not be afraid, Mary, for you have found favor with God. And now, you will conceive in your womb and bear a son, and you will name him Jesus. He will be great, and will be called the Son of the Most High, and the Lord God will give to him the throne of his ancestor David. He will reign over the house of Jacob forever, and of his kingdom there will be no end."

Stillness. There's a catch here, and Mary knows it. "Just how can this be, since I've never been with a man?" The stars stop their twinkling, the planets hesitate in their wheeling, the comets leave off flashing through the heavens, and Gabriel gives that awful, frightful answer, "The Holy Spirit will come upon you, and the power of the Most High will overshadow you; therefore the child to be born will be holy; he will be called Son of God." The angel doesn't stop there; the angel's saying something about Elizabeth, about God's power to do what's impossible, but no one is listening. Now the whole creation stands still, the universe from one end to another holds its living breath for a moment. Now everything flashes through Mary's mind, all the pain and confusion and fear and hope and wonder of it, these all rush through her heart and all of us, in every generation from Adam and Eve to the saints of the last days, we all look at this country girl and listen. Now, sisters and brothers, God Almighty sits back and waits for permission from a teenager in some Galilean backwater.

And *she* says, "Here I am, the servant of the Lord; *let it be.*" And that Gabriel leapt right back up to heaven, singing for joy.

Oh, there's something coming, all right. Something good and big and righteous, something so good we can't handle it all by ourselves. We have a gift coming that's so big we've *got* to share it. We have a gift coming that's so tremendous that we have to pass it around to friends and relatives, we even have to find strangers to pass it along to. It's a gift that we can't enjoy till we've brought in *everyone* to share it with us. Is there anyone out there on the street? *Bring them in!* Is there someone sleeping at home? *Bring them in!* Bring them in, everyone you can find, everyone who's willing to come and see. The moment is coming near, but there's still time—the clocks are still in slow motion. That woman is coming along, but the baby's not here yet. Come back Christmas Eve, wait with us, and bring someone along—so that together we may share the revelation of the mystery that was kept secret for long ages but is now disclosed, and through the prophetic writings is made known to all the Gentiles, according to the command of the eternal God, to bring about the obedience of faith—to the only wise God, through Jesus Christ, to whom be the glory forever!

4 LENT

2 Chronicles 36:14-23; Ps 122; Eph 2:4-10; John 6:4-15

I was glad when they said to me, "Let us go to the house of the Lord."

In the Name of God Almighty,
                      the Blessed Trinity on high— **Amen.**

    I will confess that there are days, actually usually there are *evenings*, when Margaret and I are not thinking in perfect harmony. Usually such times arise when we've each had a wearying day, we feel acutely how much we have yielded, how much *we* have earned soothing consideration, and even a little indulgence, and at those times each of us senses that our spouse and our children are insufficiently attentive to our injured condition. Somewhat sulkily, we will prepare dinner or wash the dishes, until some off-hand cue provides one of us the opportunity to let our frustrations and annoyances out, the gloves are off, and we need to let off a considerable quantity of steam. In such circumstances, so far as I can tell, we are equally aware (in some way) that we both have put up with undue nonsense in our days, that there's no real way that two wounded weary hearts can find in themselves the new strength to overflow with compassion and clemency for another, to show one another the grace that we both need. That's because in some recess of our spirits, we both are firmly convinced that *we're* the especially injured party.

    "Pray for the peace of Jerusalem; may they prosper who love you."

    Diplomats haggle over which suburb constitutes a part of the ancient holy city, ideologues bluster and threaten, and compromising politicians try to create the illusion that *they* and they alone have brokered a transient calm in the simmering hostilities of the Mid-East. Several communities of residents each clamor that *they* have suffered the most grievous wounds of history, that they merit special treatment even at the expense of their neighbors. We pray for the peace of Jerusalem, indeed; but we can hardly see how, when everyone has suffered injustice, any settlement has much chance to be *fair* to everyone. Among injured, embittered people, what is the way to peace?

The Psalmist says, "Pray." Where a practical observer might expect that the road to peace lies by way of negotiation, bargains, compromise, and deal-cutting, the psalm reminds us, "Pray." Where someone might mandate the necessity of direct political action, we hear the psalm affirm that "Because of the House of the Lord, I will seek to do you good." This morning, a congregation of active, empowered, *effective* Christians, eager to demonstrate their faith by taking affairs into their hands, by putting their energies toward setting things right, sings a reminder that prayer lays the roadbed on the path toward peace.

Now, the psalmist and I, we are not commending cursory recitation as a panacea, any more than you might suggest that a Mid-East peace treaty could be settled with a little marketplace haggling. The wounds are so deep, the memories even of long-past wrongs are so vivid, that only the most arduous of prayers befits the work of peace. Our all-too-human impulsive willingness to inflict hurt has wrought so much harm that we can only *begin* to be undone by serious prayer, painstaking penitence, by searching our souls for a truth that may hurt us every bit as much as our adversaries have hurt us; perhaps the truth will hurt us even more.

That is one measure of peace: our willingness to swallow hard and accept our complicity in ways of living, talking, arguing, politicking, that injure our sisters and brothers. We don't need to tear out our hair, to moan and abase ourselves, to look from West Jerusalem to East and say, "I am sorry for the wrongs that I have done." Our will to come out on top tends to mask itself as a will to achieve justice for ourselves; yet the same will that clings fast to our rightly *deserving* a bigger share of concessions, a lighter load of responsibility, is the will that insists that there is not enough bread to go around, so that other people must go without in order to accommodate our needs. As long as that will is in charge, as long as someone else pays the price of my satisfaction, while anybody's *I* sets the standard of deserving, we may attain brief pauses between flare-ups, but we will not know peace. Peace will come only through giving.

I can't recommend that any one here give so freely. I can't tell someone else to spill their heart's blood to offer reconciliation to their enemies; I haven't felt their suffering, I don't know your disappointment and betrayal. What I can do is to stand up for the truth, to read aloud the words of Scripture that remind us how the way of peace was prepared for us by Jesus, who himself walked into the teeth of hostility, who stood by the truth even when it cost his life, who called us to follow after him and promised us immeasurable riches and true peace: peace to those who were far off, and peace to those who are near. He made a way for us where no way had led before, a harmonious path of reconciliation and unity. In Christ's way of peace, our family's and our companions' well-being are most deeply strengthened and affirmed when we pass the bread along to others, when we pray for our neighbors, when we take care of others' neediness without calculating how much they deserve.

That is the very good work for which we are created in Christ Jesus—the prayerful labor of making Christ known—Christ who *is* our peace, who breaks down every dividing wall of hostility. But one can't walk in those good works, indeed, one can't even begin to pray properly so long as their hearts are directed not toward the glory of God's praise, but toward keeping score of whether someone else has gotten more square inches of turf. Jerusalem is built as a city that is at unity with itself, but *we* parcel up the Holy City into quarters. How can we be glad when they say to us, "Let us go to the House of the Lord," if every step of the way demarcates our divisions against one another? Jew, Muslim, and Christian all claim they go up to Jerusalem to praise the Name of the Lord, but how can God hear our prayers when with the same tongue we curse our neighbors? Our God is a God of plenty, whose justice made known to us in grace, forgiveness and generosity; we who had been dead in our hostility and sin, who have been made alive together with Christ—by grace we have been saved!—we must find some way of turning our lives from gloomy mirrors of human fear and scarcity to transparent windows onto God's divine love and superabundance.

The Psalmist blessed Jerusalem because in it stood the Temple, the Holy of Holies, the house of the Lord our God. That temple stands no longer; its very ruins have been scattered. Yet we may still build a house for God, a house of welcome and peace, to which we go up gladly indeed. At this moment, our love and forgiveness for one another builds up and supports the walls of that holy house. Right here is Jerusalem; right here is the house of the Lord. Now our very feet are standing at the threshold of God's sacred presence. The air is charged with sacred fire, our words of steel are chased with divine gold, our hymns elevated by the choirs of angels who join with us in singing praise. In this house of God, our penitence balks the forces of bitterness and God's forgiving grace holds at bay the demons of mistrust and suspicion. Because of the house of the Lord our God, we will seek to do good, to pass the bread along. With the power of God nearly palpable in the air that *fills* St. Luke's Church, we dare to call upon the Name of God, before the witnesses of Luke and Mary, of Agnes, Athanasius, Columba and Augustine, of angels and saints, of a congregation that extends more than a century back in this place, a communion that reaches 'round the globe more than millennia before us—and with God, our conscience, and this great cloud of witness we pray for the peace of Jerusalem, for peace between sister and brother, wife and husband, neighbor and neighbor. We will break bread together this morning, as a pledge that we will not cease loving, forgiving, sharing, comforting, offering even *enemies* the abundant grace God has shown us, until God's house, not built by human hands but by the sheer power of holiness, shelters us all. God forgive us; God bless us; God bring us together, in Jerusalem.

2 LENT

Genesis 22:1-14; Romans 8:31-39; Mark 8:31-38

Peter took Jesus aside and began to rebuke him. But turning and looking at his disciples, Jesus rebuked Peter and said, "Get behind me, Satan! For you are setting your mind not on divine things but on human things."

In the Name of God Almighty,
          the Blessed Trinity on High— *Amen.*

  Are you afraid to talk about sin?

  I raise the question because in my forays onto the information superhighway, one of the factoids people want loudly to assert about Episcopalians is that they are afraid to talk about sin, that they have abandoned the notion that there might be anything wrong with people, and that all Episcopalians want is to make everyone feel mushy, warm sentiments of inclusivity and acceptance. This came as something of a surprise to me; I haven't felt mushily warm and accepted in a long time. But because I don't want to seem out of touch with what's happening now, I turn the question around to you: are you afraid to talk about sin?

  I confess that I'm not. I talk about sin rather a lot (though I don't usually call people "Satan"). Perhaps I shouldn't, but it seems to me that if one isn't willing to talk about sin, then there isn't much of anything left to say about the rather horrible condition of the world. Surely one must be able to name sin in a world where it doesn't even shock us to hear that one group of human beings is besieging another group, slowly starving, freezing them to death, killing thousands of unarmed civilians; surely we recognize sin in a world where the wicked prosper and the righteous suffer; surely we can't be ashamed to talk about sin in a world where the light of Christ is constantly eclipsed by the hideous misdeeds of Christians. If Christians are embarrassed to talk about sin in this kind of world, what on earth else do they have to talk about?

But I think that there's more at stake here than just sin-in-general; I think that the prophets on the electronic bulletin boards want to rebuke Episcopalians because there are *certain specific sins* that we don't talk about as often they'd like. And that's a very different matter indeed.

But let us boldly go ahead and talk about specific sins. Let us name one sin in particular. It is a sin which the church long condemned from its pulpits. It is a sin which is clearly *de*scribed and *pro*scribed in the books of Exodus, Leviticus, and Deuteronomy. It is a sin which our modern permissive atmosphere has made us hesitate to name, to the point now where bishops, priests, deacons, and lay people practice this sin without hesitating. Let us name boldly the sin of *lending at interest*.

The principle of lending money for interest is opposed to biblical principles about the right use of resources and the right social order of God's people, whether it is our lending our savings to a bank for interest, or a bank's lending money to us for a mortgage, or a car loan, or an educational loan. The whole principle of the Jubilee year, in which slaves were released and debts were erased, was that those of us who have more money than we need at the moment should willingly use that money to help our less fortunate sisters and brothers—and not by any means for profit: Moses specifically commands Israel, "If you lend money to my people, to the poor among you, you shall not deal with them as a creditor; you shall not exact interest from them" (Ex 20:25), and again, "You shall not charge interest on loans to another Israelite, interest on money, interest on provisions, interest on anything that is lent" (Dt 23:19). And Jesus specifically insists, "Lend, expecting nothing in return. Your reward will be great, and you will be children of the Most High" (Lk 6:34f). The people of God are called not to extract profit from one another, but to help one another.

The early church shared this abhorrence of charging interest, and it became an assumption of medieval Christianity that money-lenders were inherently evil. One theological poem of the fourteenth century goes so far as to warn Christians not to accept any gift or favor in return for a loan:

O brother, hold fast to these words every day:
For many of those *called* Christian men today
Conceal such usury as slyly as they may.
They will not loan purely for God's benediction
But for gift or service, favor or promotion.
Such folk sin highly, God's word not pondering:
"Give your loan, thereof no interest hoping."
Else God will chase you far from the heaven on high
And erase your name from the book of endless life...

    The church came to terms with the practice of lending money for interest when the people started to think that interest wasn't really all *that* bad, that times had changed since Moses' law, that Christ had freed us from the Old Testament's injunctions against such profit, and that Christ's counsel against profiting from another person's need was only a *spiritual* teaching. When ours became a money-lending society, the church found that money-lending wasn't all that bad. The church turned its back on Scripture, including the specific teachings of Jesus, and on its own tradition, in order to bless a kind of behavior we had hitherto regarded as sin.

    You see, I'm not afraid to talk about sin. In fact, I think we *need* to talk about sin, all the time; because if we don't *talk* about sin, it's easy to to fall into the habit of thinking of "sin" as a big list of things you might do wrong. But sin is much more than a list of possible offenses; sin is the human tendency to justify *whatever* we want to do. Sin is the tendency to put *our* desires in the place of *God's will* for us. Like Peter, we try to tell Jesus how he ought to go about this salvation business; we want God not only to forgive and save us, but to save us *on our own terms*.

    The problem we have is that people afflicted by sin—people like you and me—are not in the best position to make decisions about what constitutes good behavior. Part of the whole idea of sin is that sin clouds our capacity to discern what's right and wrong.

    So we need *frequently* to talk about sin, argue about sin, make prayerful decisions about what kinds of behavior we honor and which we condemn, because the people of God learn to discern the truth from falsity and error by talking, praying, confessing, working, deliberating with one another. After all, we are taught that not all spirits are good, not all truths build us up and strengthen us, so we are called to *test* the spirits.

As we discuss and argue and test the spirits, we pray for the guidance of the Holy Spirit, whom we trust to lead us into all truth. We pray for patience and forgiveness, because sometimes our heartfelt convictions arise from our own short-sightedness or selfish interests rather than from God's testimony in our hearts. In that process, we sometimes find that our ancestors and Scripture have something to teach us about how we order our lives. And sometimes we even discover that actions our ancestors thought were inherently sinful are no more harmful than getting 3% interest on your retirement account at the credit union.

Peter thought he knew all about God's plan. Peter, our own St. Peter, thought he was in a position to dictate to Jesus how to save us, how to be the messiah. And just when Peter was most confident about what God wanted, Jesus lashed out at him: "Get behind me, Satan!" Peter had to find out that no matter what he had learned from Scripture, no matter what he's learned from his teachers, no matter what the leading theologians decreed, his vision was clouded with sin. His convictions about salvation were all wrong. Jesus was going to save people *God's* way, not Peter's way.

That illustrates the trouble with sin: it is most dangerous to us when we're surest of ourselves, when we're least open to the possibility that we're sinning. Indeed, some of the electronic prophets on the information superhighway are unalterably certain that God is on their side, that they can assuredly rebuke other people with the authority of God. Maybe they are right. But when you claim to know God's business, you are setting yourself up for the most grievous fall; you run the risk of being found on the side of Satan, not on God's side.

There's no infallible way to avoid that danger; we are all inescapably entangled in treacherous swamps of sin, and no one can just leap out of his or her sin to give us an undistorted report about exactly what's right or wrong. But if we will remember to talk with each other about sin, and especially to *listen* patiently to each other about sin, then we can come before God to pray for forgiveness with a truer sense that we recognize our *own* sinfulness. And I trust that when we listen to one another patiently and honestly, when we confess our sin, we will learn from one another a Lenten discipline which runs deeper than anything I read about on the internet. We will be bound together inseparably in patient, penitent, trusting love, in the name of God.

PENTECOST

Acts 2:1-11; 1 Corinthians 12:4-13; John 20:19-23

When the day of Pentecost had come, they were all together in one place. And suddenly a sound came from heaven like the rush of a mighty wind, and it filled all the house where they were sitting. And there appeared to them tongues of fire, distributed and resting on each one of them. And they were all filled with the Holy Spirit, and began to speak in other tongues. . . .

In the Name of God, Father, Son, and Holy Spirit— *Amen.*

    The Feast of the Pentecost revealed the power of the Holy Spirit among the apostles for the first time. St. Luke describes it for us as a spectacular scene—rushing winds, a fiery light show, apostles speaking strange languages which at the same time everyone who heard could understand. This first manifestation of the Holy Spirit set the stage for the explosive growth of the early Church, a growth which crossed the boundaries of nations and continents, and which the first believers saw was undeniably the work of the Holy Spirit. That Pentecost was an exhilarating illustration of what wonders can come when Spirit-filled followers of the Christ come together to do God's work. But perhaps it would be a better thing if we never had heard this story.
    It might be better for all of us if we never knew that the Holy Spirit can so take over our tongues that we can communicate the Gospel of God's love and justice to our sisters and brothers, no matter what language they speak. Maybe we shouldn't even know that the Spirit can rush through our lives like a whirlwind, like a tornado, picking us up in one spot and dumping us somewhere we didn't expect to be. Perhaps we're too small to know that there was a time and a place where you could see the Spirit burning in believers. Because once we know this story, once we have heard about the glorious display and the astonishing sound effects and the miraculous gift of spiritual

translation, then we descendants of the apostles tend to want not their work, nor even their gifts, but we want their glory.

So I want to promise you this morning, my sisters and brothers, that the holy feast of the Church's first Pentecost is not about any of the marvels which can so grasp our attention. There is no spiritual benefit in just having your hair on fire, or in being in the middle of a tornado, or even in jabbering in languages you've never heard of before. These things can happen apart from the Holy Spirit—they can even be signs of the most evil of spirits. If we latch onto the special effects part of the Pentecost story—as exciting and enthralling as it is—then we have missed the substance of that event. We have bought the sizzle instead of the steak, and we will go away malnourished.

The fire we need to seek is the fire in the hands of a nurse, or in the heart of a poet, the fire which fuels the athlete's endurance and excellence. Though there be no tongues of flame when these exercise their vocation, yet we must be sure that theirs are gifts of the Holy Spirit. The fire which drives those who govern well to legislate on behalf of their oppressed and neglected constituents, that fire burns with a holy brightness. The Spirit's fire burns in the conscience of a penitent sinner, scorching the memories and impulses which glamorize exploitation, and selfishness; it is the Spirit's fire which forges in believers a new, purer, stronger heart. Those who see us turn away from the idols of consumerism—greed, self-indulgence, indiscriminate sexuality—will not observe dancing flames over our heads; some congregations which prize the external display of spiritual gifts might not be impressed at the hidden fire with which Spirit fuels the vocation of nurse, poet, athlete, the hidden fire which cleanses the sinner's conscience; but all these are to be prized above all dramatic flaming special effects.

The rushing wind we need to seek out is the irresistible power of the God, which drives out injustice and overturns the structures of tyranny. When the people of God come together with their hearts set on righteousness, when they assemble to praise the God who comforts the poor and the afflicted, who sets the captive free, then the power of the Spirit moves among them with a force no hurricane can match. The rushing power of the

Holy Spirit is let loose among those who teach their children, their neighbors, their sisters and brothers that our God is a God who loves believers fiercely, who imparts to them a dignity which no power or principality can strip from them. There is no greater manifestation of the Spirit than that which we see when a believer trusts God to protect her, and resolutely faces the dangers which inevitably await those who resist evil armed only with their faith in the Lamb who was slain. Walking together for social change, teaching others the truth of God's ennobling love for us, risking mortal life to resist evil—these are not the spiritual gifts we think of when we read about the apostles' thrilling Pentecostal wind. Yet if we forego the irresistible power of the Spirit, no gusting wind, no hurtling tornado can mark us as followers of our Savior.

And what manifestation of exotic tongues can compare with the overwhelming power of a child's prayer? The Spirit's gift of tongues appears among us when the faithful speak out on behalf of those who have no voices in our culture. We hear the strange language of the Spirit when prophets remind us of sins to which we had become accustomed, when preachers move our hearts to feel God's claim on our lives more keenly than ever, when a congregation joins together to say, "Our Father," and "Alleluia! Thanks be to God!" The Spirit's language is the language of heartfelt love, the love which draws two souls ever closer to one another. If none of these is as startling or as newsworthy as the apostles' speech on that first Pentecost, yet we must recognize that the gifts of the Spirit run deeper than TV news's sound bites, they take longer to explain than a paragraph in *USA Today*. The gift of tongues comes not principally in cases of tongue-speaking, but above all when our words, when all our communication makes the Gospel of love and truth clearer to those around us.

There is no reason to disdain the manifestations of the Spirit at that first Pentecost. Tongue-speaking isn't a bad thing, nor are visions of heavenly fire, nor the sounds of a rushing wind. But we live among people who have been sold the idea that only the superficial is important, only the simple is true, only the obvious is deep, only the pleasurable is good, only the gratifying is right.

Sometimes we fall for those lies ourselves. And among people who think that way, in a time in a land which advertises those *dis*-values as its own gospel, we must remember that there's a land of difference between an exciting show and the transformation which comes from the indwelling presence of the Holy Spirit. We must remember the the Spirit brings comfort, challenges, strength, risks, skills, obligations, love, and pain more often than it brings flashing lights and roaring sound. Our words speak the strange tongue of a Spirit which is foreign to our culture; our works must burn with the strange fire of a Spirit which sears away what our neighbors think is most precious; our lives must testify to the unyielding power of the Spirit which will not abandon God's people to poverty, injustice, exclusion, and destruction. For these gifts of the Spirit speak more persuasively, burn more brightly, and roar more forcefully even than the Spirit's gifts on that day in Jerusalem. For the courage to seek out these gifts, we pray to the Lord this Pentecost morning, and every morning.

PROPER 7

Job 38:1-11, 16-18; 2 Corinthians 5:14-21; Mark 4:35-5:20

Then the Lord answered Job out of the whirlwind....

In the name of God: Variegated Unity
               and Undivided Trinity—*Amen.*

Job is up against serious odds. Here he is, lonely, afflicted, bereft of children and stuck with unhelpful nosey neighbors, proclaiming his innocence and righteousness—and right at *this* moment, as if Job weren't in a tough enough spot, God steps into the discussion.

"*Who are you*, darkening counsel by words without knowledge? Gird up your loins like a *man*, and I will question you." Plenty of people—maybe some of you, sisters and brothers—plenty of people will protest that God is beating up on Job at this moment. Mercy sakes alive, he's at the bottom of the heap, he's a homeless beggar, he's moaning the blues by the city gate, and as if he doesn't have enough trouble, a *whirlwind* sweeps down on him, and suddenly God's going to cross-examine him. The God of these verses sounds like an pitiless bully; even if we grant that God's about to give Job back his house and property, all his possessions, and a new, improved set of children, it looks as though God is just plain tormenting Job at a time when Job *doesn't need* any additional troubles. In a primordial version of "Who Wants to be a Millionaire?" God plays the Quizmaster and Job is stuck trying to answer questions like, "Where were you when I laid the foundation of the earth? Tell me, if you have understanding. Who determined its measurements—surely *you* know!" And we stand by in embarrassed silence; we don't know the answers, but we feel an awful sympathy for our brother Job's predicament. We wish God wouldn't pick on him that way.

Now, God does not need me to serve as the divine Press Secretary. That's the kind of presumption that gets Elihu and

Zophar and Eliphaz and Bildad the Shuhite into trouble at the end of the story. But we might want to look closely before we indict God on charges of harassment and brutality. Job did, after all, invite God to play this guessing-game with him. All through the book, up to the beginning of the lesson this morning, everything Job said has been setting the scene for this face-to-whirlwind confrontation. Twenty-four chapters back, Job said, "I would speak to the Almighty, and I desire to argue my case before God." (*Whoops.*) Job said, "Call, and I will answer. Let me speak, and *you* reply to *me*." (*Oh.*) So when God makes this dramatic entrance and starts interrogating Job—Job is only getting what he *specifically* asked for.

But it still seems—oh, I don't know—*excessive*. It seems like overkill. Why can't God just poke Job in the ribs from out of the whirlwind, and gently say, "Let me handle this one"?

I suppose God could have. But maybe the point isn't just that God has everything wired—that God has power over the foundations of the earth, over the stars in the heavens, over the seas and all this is in them, but maybe Job has understood God wrong in a way that the very tone of these verses picks up and *reflects back* to him. Job and his buddies are working out of the habit of thinking that God won't allow any bad thing ever to happen if you behave yourself, that God will make a personal appearance to fend off the Category-Four hurricane from the houses of kind-hearted Floridians, but will steer the destroying winds *toward* the homes of the assassins and the corrupt politicians. Job and his posse are working with a Superman theology, and Job is there by the roadside with a big-time spiritual flat tire, waiting for a divine Triple-A truck to roll up and fix his life. And as Job stands waving his arms, shouting, trying to get the attention of God—God answers him.

Sisters and brothers, as a professional in the field of education, indeed of *theological* education, I can alert you that you may not want to try this at home. There are ways to learn about God that do not entail poverty, boils, and the annihilation of your immediate family. Indeed, Job seems himself to have missed the point: if he can be confident that his redeemer liveth, and that at the end he will be acquitted and he will see God on his side, then maybe there's something *else* going on than a simple reward-for-goodness, punishment-for-badness equation. Maybe, however hard it is for Job and us to hear, grace is at work even when times are hardest.

For that's at least one part of what's happening in the whirlwind this morning. God is reminding Job of Job's very own words:

> Where shall wisdom be found?
> And where is the place of understanding?
> Mortals do not know the way to it,
> and it is not found in the land of the living.
> The deep says, "It's not in me"
> and the sea says, "Now with me.". . .
> *God* understands the way to wisdom,
> and *God* knows its place, and said to humankind,
> "Truly, the fear of the Lord, that is wisdom. . . ."

That's "fear of the Lord" not in the sense of being frightened, scared of a big, tough Deity, but "fear of the Lord" as in "experiencing the awe that comes with recognizing God's unnerving, surpassing beauty and greatness." Wisdom begins as we worship the Lord in the beauty of holiness, not when we try to hide from God, and not when we demand that God meet us on our own terms. Our sympathy for the poor soul against whom everything has gone wrong can make God's questions to Job resound with mockery and sarcasm—but these same questions are just as much an appeal for Job to remember what Job himself has already said. God's begging Job to pick up the clue phone and *remember*.

What should Job remember? Job should remember—and *we* should remember—that the way of this world and the way of God—as Paul says, "knowing from a human point of view" and "knowing from a divine point of view"—these ways cross and intersect, they run parallel and diverge, but they are not the *same* way. The path to the truth is not an arithmetical path from a few simple propositions to a logical conclusion. The way of God is not just the way of authentic personhood, only with a more ethereal soundtrack. The route to wisdom doesn't end with righteousness alone. Job *had* that. It's Job's *righteousness* that's the stumbling-block.

The way to wisdom is a dizzying, fearsome path through death to life. Righteousness is good; no doubt about it, God wishes us righteous and true and just. But more than God wants us to be righteous, God wants us to be *here,* coming together with our sisters and brothers, bringing our varied gifts to enact our identity as the body of Christ—Christ's body not from a human point of view, but from the point of view of the God who loved Jesus, and who loves us as we are so that, in Christ, we can become something new. And if we cling too tightly to our righteousness—or if we dread coming before God without enough righteousness—we, like Job, miss the point.

"Where were you when I laid the foundation of the earth? Who determined its measurements—surely you know!" We weren't there, we don't know who measured the universe, what we know is the pain and disappointment we feel when our lives are out of control and all we have to hang onto is our *own righteousness*—but even then Job can turn, *we* can turn, and embrace the whirlwind God who loves us through our suffering, who draws together into a hope that our friends can offer us even when we don't feel it ourselves. But we don't *have* to feel that hope for ourselves, we don't have to know the right answers, we don't have to nail down a righteousness of our own. God has provided hope and wisdom and righteousness for us, and offers them to us in the Body of Christ.

God calls us to righteousness; God calls us to wisdom; but at the deepest heart of the foundations of all things, God is calling to us to come forward, to come out, to come together, *now.* God has made everything ready for us, has made *us* ready, so that we might receive the precious gift of God's presence in us, in our heart and in our soul. God has *appointed* us *ambassadors* of the New Creation. And here is the only answer we need: When we come forward to receive God—present for us, made visible here in a few morsels of bread, a drop of wine—when we take these in remembrance that we *become* the living Body of Christ, the very righteousness of God, then our answer is:

Amen

WORLD AIDS DAY

Psalm 55

This afternoon, I bring you messages from the AIDS Memorial Quilt. I have spent much of the last few weeks in San Francisco studying Quilt panels, reading, taking notes, and sometimes crying. So this is my first message to you all: I wish you well, sisters and brothers, as I bring you greetings and appreciation from the national office of the NAMES Project Foundation, the custodians of the AIDS Quilt. I wish I could say that their work is going well, that spirits at the Foundation are strong, but recent social and medical developments have cut into support for the Quilt; while we give many thanks that HIV-infected people now have a chance to live longer and more comfortably, the AIDS crisis is far from being over. Your prayers, your volunteer time, your contributions, and your commitment to fighting for a better, safer, fairer, healthier world are as important now as they ever have been, and in San Francisco your efforts are recognized and deeply appreciated. That's my first message from the Quilt: Thank you, and God bless you, and keep pressing on.

My second message from the Quilt:

> Jack—
> While you were out
> Gordon died
>   Signed, Gert

Third message from the Quilt, from William Davis Austin: "Even in the final months of his illness Bill would say, 'I'm so lucky, I've had it all.' Of course, it may be that Bill was no luckier than the rest of us, except he had the ultimate wisdom to know he was blessed and to live every day of his life in awe and with gratitude." Or from another panel:

> To you who are still alive,
> What is important?
> And while you are still alive,
> what are you doing about it?
> Love, Patrick H. LeBlanc

Sisters and brothers, one reason I am here with you this afternoon is the number of times I've had the privilege of being taught by friends with HIV. There is much to learn in our complicated world, and some of my friends have been strong and wise and generous enough to reach out to this academic priest who thought *he* was ministering to *them*. Gary used to promise me that his infection was the best thing that ever happened to him. Many other people living with AIDS assured me that they had no regrets; that they never saw so clearly, loved so richly or selflessly, that they never before had known what life was about until they came to terms with death. I think Jack was the first one to remind me, "We're both dying, you and me. The difference is that *I* know it, and *you* don't." So my third message reminds us that no one dies from AIDS; people with AIDS die of the same kinds of thing that you and I will die from, but sooner.

Fourth message from the Quilt comes from an anonymous panel: "This disease is hell." I occasionally hear someone observe that such-and-such a person with AIDS "died for us," died to bring us insight or appreciation or retrospective understanding. That always makes me furious. We who will live a little longer must *never* romanticize or paint over or perfume the suffering and pain that give rise to the generous grace I just described. There has been too much agony, the wisdom has been far too costly, for us to cash it in cheaply and admire smiley Polaroids of the saintly departed. Glenn King's panel reminds us,

> They said, "Friends will die."
> I cringed.
> They said, "Warriors fight best."
> I changed.
> They said, "Some will be wounded."
> I bled.

They said, "To die is glorious."
They lied.

Jeff McMullen's panel has a similar message for us:

> You see a little chip on my shoulder,
> I'm surprised it isn't a boulder.
> If a tear could possibly fall
> it would turn to solid ice.
> I work hard to be cordial
> so don't expect me to be nice.
> Just Don't Hate Me!
> I won't ask you to join in my fight
> or expect to see you in this war.
> Alone. . . still curse
> the day I was born.

Susan's panel makes the point more poignantly:

> The summer I first developed "symptoms"
> I began what I called my "June Cleaver psychosis"
> On good days, inviting a multitude of kids in
> For sandwiches and cookies
> Tempted to believe that
> A shirtwaist dress and apron and the preparation of food
> Might ward off the virus like a cross does a vampire.
>
> At Hanukah the following winter
> As blood counts dwindled and surgery loomed closer
> I invited a family of six, at the last minute, for potato latkes
> Relishing the anxiety of not being able to grate
>   enough potatoes
> in time
> I magically produced the golden latkes
> A good stand-in for the blood platelets I was unable to
>   maintain.

This week, when a friend was sick and dying,
And my own fear filled me with helplessness
At seven one morning
I prepared a pot of chicken soup to deliver
Believing that it contained the healing rituals passed on to me
By my mother and grandmother
The joy of feeding so genetically a part of me
More potent than any stress-management activity.

I have an ongoing fantasy
That someday the *New England Journal of Medicine*
Will publish an article about "phase 3 testing"
Showing "promising results" both anti-viral and
                                       immune boosting
From warm chocolate chip cookies
Fresh out of the oven
Chocolate melting on the tongue like holy-wafers
Out performing AZT and pentamadine
Brimming with non-toxicity
and sweetness
and joy
And "irrefutable clinical evidence"
That these cookies can immobilize the virus
And restore T-cell counts to normal levels.

Many who have died with AIDS have had the great grace to share with us some blessings they found along the way, but there's a big difference between receiving a gift from a dying friend, and presuming to say that our friends "died for us," that their deaths have meaning because they enrich our lives. Jerry didn't die for me; he died because, twelve years into a lethal epidemic, the most medically-sophisticated culture in the world was still only *beginning* to study treatments for a condition that goes on infecting a greater and greater portion of the world's people. David's life doesn't "have meaning" because he left a message that would change my life; his life has meaning because he knew love, he shared that love with others, and he reached out to a society that shunned him and his brothers, and offered it a gift of beauty and wisdom. Fourth message from the Quilt: We, the heirs of our friends and loved ones, remember their names, cherish their lives, and we will not diminish Jerry and David by fashioning their suffering into a cheap consolation for us who survive. Our insights are too small, and their deaths too costly; if we say, "they died for us," we either inflate our own importance or we cheapen their deaths.

The fifth message comes from Doug's panel:

[AIDS] cannot cripple love
It cannot shatter hope
It cannot corrode faith
It cannot eat away peace
It cannot destroy confidence
It cannot kill freindship [*sic*]
It cannot shout out memories
It cannot silence courage
It cannot reduce eternal life
It cannot quench the spirit
It cannot invade the soul or the love we have for you

Faith, hope, love, peace, confidence, friendship, memories, courage; everything depends on sustaining these graces, in our own lives and especially in the lives of our brothers and sisters who have HIV or AIDS. Illness and death can only triumph if we relinquish faith, hope, and love; so long as we persevere in trusting, in hoping, in loving one another in this life and beyond it, illness has won no victory, and death has simply deferred a reunion that will ultimately transcend the horizons of mortality.

Sixth message: Fred Riehm and Bob Folkman say this:

Here We Sleep • Beneath These Covers • But We Are Not At Rest • Contained Within This Quilt Is A Packet of Our Ashes. • Let It Serve As A Reminder To You, The Living, That Your Work Is Not Yet Done. • We Urge You This: Find The Cure. And When You Do, Come Back To This Panel And Set Us Free.

Fred and Bob are not free so long as any of our sisters and brothers are at risk for infection. Fred and Bob are not yet free, and so long as Fred and Bob aren't free, *we* are not free: our hearts are bound in obligation to our loved ones who have died. We are not free to shrug off their lives. We are not free simply to miss them without taking action on behalf of others. Protease inhibitors and three-drug cocktails are wonderful, but they do not release us; they're available only to relatively few people, most of them in this land of privilege; they do not *cure* those who rely on them, and in an uncomfortable number of cases even this best course of medication fails. *We are not free* until all our sisters and brothers are free. That's one reason we gather here today; not everyone is a research biochemist or pharmacologist, not everyone can send money or lean on a politician, some of us can and must to these things, and the rest of us, indeed, we *all* can show our commitment to Fred Riehm and Bob Folkman in the ways we live, in the people we help, in the gifts we give and the help we offer. Italo Tulipano entreats us: "Pray Always." We who have been changed by the AIDS crisis can't just pretend it never happened; we can't keep from speaking out, from speaking up, and some of us can't keep from *acting up* when our friends and lovers and sisters and brothers are at risk of being forgotten. We can't stop praying. We are people who remember their names—and we are not free to let the world forget, we are not free to let the rich and powerful rest easy, we are committed to testifying to their precious lives, their bruised souls, to their sacred trust in us.

The seventh, and final, message—from the panel for Charles Engstrand:

Dean?
8:30 AM
(Yes honey).
I'm hearing beautiful music. . .
(Do you, honey lamb?)
(What else, my love?)
"Yes. . . Red ones . . . Green ones . . . Yellow ones."
(That's wonderful honey—walk toward the light)

8:56 AM
(I will wait to see you again.)

This is why we are not free—because we are waiting to see our loved ones again, and we want to be able to look Charles and Doug and Glenn and Jeff and Fred and Bob in the eyes when we say, "We've been praying for you; we've been waiting for you; we've remembered your name. " Or when we say together the words of Bill Devino & John Wiggs's panel: "Love conquers all, and with our prayers, Love will triumph over this plague. We will keep the love alive."

GOOD FRIDAY

Father, forgive them, for they do not know what they are doing.

In the Name of God Almighty,
        the Blessed Trinity on High— *Amen.*

I know a whole lot. I know the sweet kiss of a drowsy child, the scintillating misty hush of a summer sunrise. I know uses of the Greek participle, I know the forlorn plaints from the trampled heart of a student, a friend, a lonely visitor to my office. I know the psalms, I know the working of a well-practiced basketball team, I know contents of the heaps of paper on my desktop. I know fear and doubt, I know pain and desperation, I know joy and pride and satisfaction. In the age of expertise, I am an expert; in the age of "just do it," I've been there and I've done that. I *know* what I am doing.

I know that we gather here this afternoon to recollect the trial of God, the day we put our Savior on trial—and executed him. Our trial of God is not in any way a presumption on our part; though we may want to demur, Jesus demands that we participate. Jesus came to Jerusalem, came here to the center of the world, and looked us in the eyes; and he asks, "Are my claims on you, on your life, on your whole being—are my claims on you just?" Today's trial comes at Jesus' own initiative, according to God's own will; however much we'd rather recuse ourselves, we may not. Oyez, oyez, oyez.

The accused is charged with bringing God's uncompromising word into human life. He stands before us, alone at the defense table, under indictment for making us feel awkward, for asking too much of us, for calling us to a way of life that puts us out of step with our more comfortable neighbors. He confesses as much; he offers no resistance to this trial. Ladies and gentlemen of the jury, I ask you to pronounce sentence: this disturbing deity must be put out of our way. For our own sake, he must be crucified.

In the book of the Wisdom of Solomon, it is written that the people said, "Let us lie in wait for the righteous man, because he is inconvenient to us and opposes our actions; he reproaches us for sins against the law, and accuses us of sins against our training. He professes to have knowledge of God, and calls himself a child of the Lord. He became to us a reproof of our thoughts; the very sight of him is a burden to us, because his manner of life is unlike that of others, and his ways are strange. Let us see if his words are true, and let us test what will happen at the end of his life; for if the righteous man is God's child, he will help him, and will deliver him from the hand of his adversaries. Let us test him with insult and torture, so that we may find out how gentle he is, and make trial of his forbearance. Let us condemn him to a shameful death, for, according to what he says, he will be protected." Thus they reasoned, but they were led astray, for their wickedness blinded them, and they did not know the secret purposes of God, nor hoped for the wages of holiness, nor discerned the prize for blameless souls.

This is what the Book of Wisdom says of people who find discipleship too inconvenient, of people who don't want God butting into their lives with unrealistic expectations or awkward obligations, who are embarrassed to be seen with a God who keeps company with a lower class of people. Now, in so fair and reverent a church as Trinity Parish, we should feel aggrieved that the Book of Wisdom moves so rapidly from being *inconvenienced* by the Righteous One to plotting his torture and murder. We are well-intentioned people who would never have such a person executed, even if he did make our lives more complicated and more awkward. Wisdom rushes us along too far, too fast. We're not that bad.

But it seems as though we don't have that intermediate choice. All we want is some peace in which to do our daily work, to enjoy ourselves on weekends; all we want is some time when we don't have to think about whether what we're doing is right. But this inconvenient Righteous One keeps walking to his cross, because our God asks us not just for an hour on Sundays, not just to avoid high-handed felony, but this God asks of us our every breath, our every thought. Our God is a zealous God, who desires our all, and who does not willingly settle for the bits and pieces that we grudgingly concede. Certainly we don't want to crucify Jesus; but if we will not invite this Righteous One into every moment of our lives, then we take our part among his judges who put him out of the way once and for all.

Can we bring ourselves to admit that when we ask for a God who permits us a little self-indulgence on the weekend that we do not know what we are asking for? Can we acknowledge that when we ask for a God who will not judge us at all, that we are rejecting the God who longs to forgive us? Can I, a modern person, a capable person, a person who knows what he's doing, confess that perhaps I don't know so much after all?

We still have time to throw ourselves on the mercy of the court, and admit we choose the sumptuous wages of exploitation instead of the wages of holiness; we grasp for the glorious prizes of our savoir-faire rather than the prize for blameless souls; we did not know the secret purposes of God.

Almighty God, maker of all things, judge of us all: remember the words of our Lord Jesus Christ, who did not hold our waywardness against us, but prayed for us: "Forgive them; they do not know what they are doing."

EASTER SUNDAY

Isaiah 25:6-9, Mark 16:1-8

They went out and fled from the tomb, for terror and amazement had seized them; and they said nothing to anyone, for they were afraid.

In the Name of the Holy and Undivided Trinity,
          One God— *Amen.*

    St. John the Evangelist tells us that after the resurrection, Jesus passed through locked doors. Our own St. Luke tells us that Jesus appeared and disappeared mysteriously, and ultimately ascended into heaven while his disciples watched in amazement. St. Matthew tells us that at the resurrection, the earth quaked and a lightning-like angel descended from heaven. And in St. Mark's gospel this morning—nothing happens. The women go to the tomb, they see a boy dressed in white. And "they went out and fled from the tomb, for terror and amazement had seized them; and they said nothing to anyone, for they were afraid."
    St. Mark's Easter women are terrified by an empty tomb and a well-dressed teenager. Where Matthew and Luke and John dress up their stories by including the shocking, stunning, dramatic miracles surrounding the resurrection, Mark tells the most unnerving version of all, by focusing on the ordinary elements of the story. No tricks—just good news, and sunshine illuminating the empty hollow of a garden tomb, and the mourning women lose their wits.
    We don't scare that easily any more. As our computer-driven special-effects machines develop finer and fancier ways to show us things we've never seen before, things we never will see except through the power of digital imaging, directors challenge one another to show us more, to be more creatively graphic, more extraordinary, more inventive than the latest extravaganza. And I

love it; I relish this new frontier of computer animation, both as a viewer and as a former computer graphics designer. (Paula and her family invited us over to see *The Matrix*—we had a great time!) Now machines stretch our capacity to see so far that we may be able to imagine even further.

But St. Mark knows something different. Mark knows that as mesmerizing as the digital effects revolution may be, the key to our response of terror and amazement lies not in what we actually see on the screen, but in what we feel in our spine, what our mind tells us cannot be, what our nerves answer with surges of adrenaline. Mark knows that the most eery part of his resurrection story is a part he can't tell straight out.

Mark can't tell us about the resurrection straight out because we've never been there. We've never had anything quite like a resurrection intrude into our lives before. We haven't witnessed resurrection, we don't have a biological explanation for it, indeed, we have a hard time even imagining resurrection. Mark's not talking about a near-death experience—this is the real thing. We don't begin to have a handle on what it means for a fully dead, 3-days-dead, "there will be an odor" dead, 100% dead person to live again. Jesus didn't fall into a deep sleep, or a coma, or a magic trance like Sleeping Beauty in a fairy tale—we're talking about Death, the undiscovered country from whose bourn no traveler returns. Jesus didn't recover unexpectedly on the operating table, or wake up refreshed after an intensely satisfying nap. Jesus was a dead man—and God raised him to life again.

Now, it could be that St. Mark just forgot to include stories about Jesus disappearing and reappearing; could be he meant to include that one about passing through locked doors, but at the last minute it slipped his mind. It could also be, though, that Mark held back from telling us about the resurrection in the same way that H.P. Lovecraft holds back from describing the horrible monsters in his short stories of terror and panic. The words and images can't communicate just how great, how awesome a mystery this is—only goosebumps and adrenaline suffice to articulate the resurrection message.

When everything is going right for us—when in the biblical expression, our heart has grown fat—when every stock rises, when everyone is our friend, when we get raises and bonuses and fancy dates with attractive escorts, when the tax department asks *us* to audit *them*, then we lose the capacity to discern all that God is doing for us. Easy living dulls the spirit; rich foods and luxury blunt our sense for the presence of God. When God tries to call us up on earthly phone lines, there's always a busy signal. The high-living, well-dressed world ties up the lines. Important jobs and great responsibilities, engrossing hobbies and rich pleasures, momentous worries and weighty obligations clog up the lines of communication so that the gospel message can't get through.

If people must inhabit that world of comfort and luxury, then all they will ever know about resurrection amounts to nothing more than cinematic special effects. They can hire digital animators to create incredibly convincing illusions that the dead are raised; they can buy products that promises us a cornucopia of blessings; they have no king but fashion, no faith but brand loyalty. Blessed are the consumers, for theirs is the kingdom of Babylon.

Down the road a ways from the pleasure palaces, by the rivers of Babylon, brokenhearted exiles laid down their harps and wept. And when the prophet promises a messianic feast, the exiles and sojourners are the ones who have ears to hear Isaiah's promise of a day when every tear will be wiped away, when the God for whom we have waited swallows up death forever. When a Messenger from God reveals the resurrection of Jesus, grieving women recognize the terrifying power that has been turned loose. Mary and Salome and the other Mary have hearts so raw, so disconsolate, that without dramatic special effects, without seeing the heavens shredded or a fiery abyss opening at their feet, just glimpsing the open cave and the clean-clothed teenager signalled to them something ominous and awesome at work. And Friday, and yesterday, we were standing with them. Yesterday we were bereft. We were widowed, we were orphaned, we were left alone at the altar; we were alone in an impenetrable darkness at twelve noon. We were more intensely alone than we have ever been before. Our Lord was taken from us; we had abandoned him, let him be dragged away to be lynched, and the mobs had done their worst. It was a long, dark Friday, and a lonely Saturday. We have walked through the valley of the shadow of death this weekend, and our spiritual senses have been heightened by grief and disappointment, by Lenten discipline and fervent prayer.

So with your mystic sight trained by forty days of fasting, you have probably already sensed that all is not as it seems in Evanston this morning. In the spirit of full disclosure, I have to tell you that, yes indeed, more is going on than meets the eye. As part of an intricate divine scheme, our liturgy this morning pulses with an unseen, unimagined energy field. Something oozes down the aisle even as I preach. Something lurks among the glorious flowers that adorn our church; there's a secret ingredient in the incense this morning, there is a brilliant deliberation at work in the music. The words of our prayers unleash a supernatural power, no, a power that is deeper than supernatural, holy rather than demonic, a power that suffuses this sacred chamber with the pure divine energy by which all things were made and through which they have their being. Just standing here and breathing, singing, listening, eating and drinking, you absorb this soul-altering presence. One puff of incense, one sweet chord from the organ, one descant or one holy prayer, one morsel of bread, one sip of wine, and you have been invaded by a divine spirit of new and unending life. This morning, sisters and brothers, the stones move! The dawn light shines! And this morning, Jesus lives!

He lives by the power of life that will not be contained by death. He lives by the power of clear light that will not be obscured or dimmed. He lives, not just in an airy and theoretical way, but in a way that we can feel. He lives, not in an imaginary way, but in a visceral way, as a discernible force in our very lives, drawing us toward the wholeness and peace for which we strive, but which we attain only as a gift from God.

That resurrection power has been turned loose in this church, my friends, this very morning. Reach out—touch it! Listen closely—hear the rustle, hear the Spirit lifting us on the shimmering harmonies of our choirs' glorious hymns, feel the walls resound with our organ's alleluias! Look into the eyes of friend and stranger, of neighbor and nemesis, look there for the sparkle of Christ's love released in our hearts!

Miracles and wonders, step aside: In the very ordinariness of an April Sunday, there is with us this morning something more than magic—something at which the forces of hostility, the forces of death, the forces of falsehood and betrayal, of exploitation, all of these falter and crumble. Some grave is empty; some boys have donned radiant apparel; and resurrection power surges through St. Luke's, through all the world, this morning. The God of life has Eastered all creation: Alleluia! Christ is risen!

6 EASTER

Deuteronomy 4:32-40; Acts 8:26-40; John 14:15-21

I, the Lord, speak the truth; I declare what is right.

In the name of God: Source, Wellspring,
                       and Water of Life—*Amen.*

    I will not soft-soap anyone this morning. I haven't sugar-coated my message to you; we've been together several weeks now, and I have not been buttering you up, setting you up for some slick sales pitch. No three-card monte up here, no shell games. This morning we need to talk about honesty and friendship; this morning we need to speak the truth.
    We need to bring this into focus, because so much of our ordinary conversational lives don't so much take the truth for granted, as they assume that we can bypass the truth in favor of a prettified, comforting delusion about the world. When we're asked "How are you doing?" etiquette forbids our saying that we hate our boss and that the stress of dealing with our obnoxious relatives threatens to unravel the already-frayed fabric of our lives. Instead, civilized society expects us to say, "Doing fine; how're you?" Polite discourse hides from the truth, and Episcopalians are sometimes too polite for their own good.
    Politeness helps people get along together, all right, but politeness also offers a selection of attractive curtains behind which to hide our real disagreements, our real frustrations, our real and important *doubts* about one another and about the God whom we gather here to worship and praise. Tact impels us just to go ahead and mouth the words, "Doing fine," or "We believe"; to nod and bow and smile and say, "God's peace be with you," when we're not so sure who this God is or what brand of peace we're inflicting on people. Let's not press issues too far; it's better just to smile nicely, and move on.
    That won't do.

That won't do this morning, because this morning God calls out for us, God *challenges* us to seek our divine Source. This morning, God invites us home, and we can't get there by diplomacy or denial or delusion; the only way to our eternal home is by way of the truth, and that's a hard way.

Telling the truth has always been a hard job. It oughtn't be; telling the truth should come easily, just saying out loud the way things are. Truth ought to be our mother tongue, should come in and out of us as naturally and unquestionably as our very breath. But it doesn't; it's *hard* to tell the truth, harder still to *live by* the truth.

From as far back as humanity can remember, our sisters and brothers have betrayed one another, cheated one another, ducked, equivocated, evaded rather than come out with true stories—and just as long, we have stoned, slandered, condemned and executed our neighbors who told unwelcome truths. Even if we *want* to be truthful (and more folks that I wish to think don't even care one way or the other), if we want to be truthful, we're aiming at a moving target. What looks true one minute doesn't look quite the same moments later. The promise we make, the vow we take on one day doesn't always keep its hold on us after days or months or years. We are not cut out for the truth, my friends; the air is *different* there, the sun is more intense.

—Which makes our communicating with God and our seeking after God all the more peculiar an enterprise. Whereas we live in misty shade, in the cloudy atmospheres of confusion and deception, our God inhabits the crystalline purity of eternity. We cannot look on the face of God and live; we avert our gaze, we stammer and hesitate; we dodge and weave. We evade, and fudge, and sometimes we lie. People want so badly to live in a comfortable, shiny happy world that we put on rose-colored glasses and make-believe that our worlds are shiny and happy and comfortable—not beautifying them to the praise of God, but pretending, to the consolation and protection of ourselves.

The only way to God is by way of the truth, the *hard* way of the truth. And the truth is that sometimes we don't know what we believe, that sometimes we hurt so deeply that we don't know which way is up or even *care*, that sometimes we have lied to ourselves, to our beloved ones, to God, because it felt easier and more comfortable than dealing with the truth.

Here is another part of the truth: God already knows this. God is not mystified by our doubts, by our wounds, by our deceptions, not as though God were an ivy-robed near-sighted professor who can deal only with abstractions and equations, never with feelings or flesh. God knows about us; God is prepared for us, as we are. God gives us a sign of that divine understanding, that utter transparency, by coming to us as our neighbor, greeting us as friend. God meets us where we are and says, "I will show you what it means to love and to trust, even though you betray me. I will show you what it means to believe in you, even though you will doubt me. I will show you what flesh is good for: healing, calming, relishing the joys of the senses, even though you will call me a glutton and a drunk. Greater love than this, no one has: to lay down one's life for one's friends. And you *are* my friends."

With that kind of truth, the gospel lays us bare just where we most want to wrap ourselves with the fig leaves of civilized culture. But we know the words of the prayer: "Almighty God, to you all hearts are open, all desires known, and from you no secrets are hid." There's no hiding place, because there's no need to hide; the smokescreens, the closets, the disguises, these all fool only ourselves—they don't deceive the God who loves the people whom we *are,* loves us so deeply and persistently that we can't defeat that love by crucifying our brother Jesus.

Jesus comes to us in the name of the God of patience, the God who *is* love—in the name of the Truth itself that knows us as only the Creator knows creation. Jesus *summons* us into shared life where we care so much about one another and about the God by whom we're united in one body, that gradually our love is perfected. Gradually we un-learn our fear. Slowly we realize that no one can hurt us so badly that we need to hurt them first, that no one's mistrust for us obliges us to mistrust them. Steadily we lose that impulse to conceal, to control others and to control our own lives, that tries to keep God at bay, that tries to *manage* ourselves; as we grow in love for our sisters and brothers, we learn from the God who loved us first that we can draw near to

God in confidence, in fearless trust, and that we have already begun the work of unfolding God's image that abides in us. We show forth God in our lives, and we recognize it more vividly in the lives of our friends.

The truth is indeed out there, and it is not pretty. The truth is terrible and fierce, powerful and uncontrollable, *and* it is our friend. *Yes*, we may be confused, *yes* we may doubt—but God waits for us to trust, instead. *Yes*, we are still susceptible to temptation and distraction—but God waits for us to attain that clarity of heart and purpose that will enable us to walk through the hard parts, to look in the face of our own shortcomings, and admit them, and press beyond them to an integrity and honesty that we hadn't known possible. God waits for us, and Jesus comes to us as our friend, to teach us and to hold our hand as we learn to walk in truth. God waits, Jesus comes, and the Holy Spirit, untamed fire of Truth, enkindles in us the thirst for love and truth that turns us from indulgence to charity. And without our precisely knowing how, without our realizing that we have come to believe, without our noticing that now we see a tattered, frightened world in all its misery—and in that very world, in its tatters and fear, we recognize the seed of glory sprouting as the green stem of summer lilies, and when some grim destroyer mows down one stem, two more push forward. Without deliberately intending to grow in faith, our love, nurtured and encouraged by God's unwavering love for us, has matured into the freedom to live in an imperfect world, without those imperfections laying claim on our souls.

We are not powerless slaves; we are not ignorant servants. Jesus has shown us what's going on in the world, and—bitter as it is, sore painful and wearying as it is—*it is our world, by God's gracious grant*, and we will not back away from it. However powerful the lures of deceit and fear, by the love of Christ we stand against them. We stand with the saints who have triumphed over fear; we stand with the Savior who has triumphed over death; we stand with the God who loves the mixed bag of good and bad that we are. We stand together, holding one another close, in the confidence that, together, we can do greater things than we can ask or imagine. We stand with

Christ, and we dare the perfidy of a treacherous power of fear to do its worst. In the name of the Lord, we speak the *truth*, together—together, we declare what is *right*.

SEMINARY BACCALAUREATE

Joshua 3:14-4:7

While all Israel were crossing over on dry ground, the priests who bore the ark of the covenant of the Lord stood on dry ground in the middle of the Jordan, until the entire nation finished crossing over the Jordan.

 From what I've heard, some mornings you feel as though it *has* taken forty long years to arrive at this meeting-place. Some of you will have calculated how many quizzes, how many exams, how many papers, how many pages of readings you have waded through. You may be looking back on long wearisome walks through scorching heat and heavy snow, wide rivers of rainy days flowing past, mornings when you've woken up, when you could only feel what a long, hard forty-year forced march it's been—especially since you *know*, you know in your heart and your bones and your flesh, that you've practically reached your goal. You can see some folks up ahead who are already scrambling up the river bank, and you can just about tell that Jordan River good-bye, get away, Jordan River, you're climbing up into Canaan land, into the Land of Promise, and make that a *double shot* of milk and honey. It's been three years, but your feet tell you that you started a lifetime ago. It's been even *less* than three years, but in just a matter of hours President Gillespie will hand you a scroll that says, "Well done, good and faithful servant; enter into the joy of your Lord." Now the wilderness is behind you; the waters of the Jordan are lapping at the feet of those Ark-carrying priests. As soon as Joshua stops talking, we can collect our degrees, let the U-Hauls roll, and begin to settle in and scope out our first ministry placements. It's time to get to work.
 So go then, my friends, with our blessings. M.Div. seniors, go out and set your hands to the vocations for which you've been preparing these many months. Th.M. students, go out fortified

now with a second portion of Princeton's academic endowments. Ph.D. students, I don't need to urge you to get out—you're already halfway through the door. Doctors of Ministry, Masters of Arts in Religious Education, *all* our degree recipients, go out from here in the power of the Spirit to spread the clear light of the truth that we're all pursuing through the confusions and gloom of a heedless world. Retiring colleagues, go from here to relish the rest promised to all those who long have toiled in this beautiful vineyard. All, go from here strengthened by everything we have learned together, encouraged by the love and the respect that hold us together. You are disciples indeed, who have been trained for the kingdom of heaven; go out and offer our world things old and things new from the treasures Princeton Theological Seminary has put at your disposal. It's time to travel light, trusting that every good thing you give away will be replenished many times over; it's time to put those treasures to work on behalf of the people of God.

I pray that among the treasures you're carrying with you, gifts that we may have helped you to understand and appreciate, among all the virtues we nurtured and refined, among all of these you know where to find hope. Believe me—from this day forward, you will have no more precious, more powerful, and possibly no more fragile treasure. I mean real, *theological* hope, not just "optimism" or "positive thinking"; I'm talking about the kind of hope that sets as its goal the things *not* seen, the kind of hope that gives us the strength to wait with patience while we persist in building up God's people, while we strive to make a way for God's way.

Begin your new ministries with the well-schooled insight and lengthy bibliography, with lively inspiration, strong with the strength that we've built up over this long wandering together. You know what's correct doctrine, you know how to parse, you know all the right counseling moves, and I've *heard* you preach. Take with you these durable gifts, thanks be to God, but don't hang on to them so tight that your grasp on hope falters, trembles, equivocates. When the exhilaration of beginning ministry encounters the intractable forces of turf conflict, institutional habit, and temperamental colleagues in ministries, then too easily the confident trust that we started to learn here stretches and thins and frays.

When theological hope faces the challenge of everyday life, the most obvious thing for us to do is to ratchet it down to a more realistic level. That's the maneuver we learn from friends and advisers who have our best interests in mind; they warn us that hope is dangerous, because it may dissolve into fantasy, because our bosses have so often sweet-talked us with a pie in the sky instead of down-to-earth help and consolation. Hope, twisted and tugged in every direction, flickers under the stress of a thousand daily demands and pressures. Hope seems so weak, it looks so empty, that feet-on-the-ground thinking pressures us to do some concrete planning instead. Now, we have to plan, it's responsible and even necessary, but it's also seductive. Plans can tempt us to think that we control circumstances, that we have the power to establish design specifications for our world. Our plans threaten to become our idols, to which we sacrifice time, money, relationships, our integrity itself, even our faith. We risk displacing our hope in a misguided exchange for agendas and timelines.

That's a bad deal, sisters and brothers; what a sad loss that would be! How else did you endure those long hours of preparation for Hebrew quizzes? How else did you survive a year of General Ministry 100? What carried you through CPE? Through all-nighters and exam periods, through junior orientation and long-winded Baccalaureate addresses, how came you here today if not by walking in hope?

Hope leads us out through the wilderness. Hope is our pillar of cloud by day, our pillar of fire by night, whereas our plans are nothing more than a hand-drawn road map with an uncertain itinerary. Hope draws us beyond what we know, what we expect, beyond what we can ask or imagine, when plans tangle us in the snarls of everyday-ness. Hope brought us out of exile, through deprivation, beyond oppression, home to grace. Hope fed us with quail and manna, hope gave us living water from the desert rock, hope whispered to us that strong topic for our dogmatics paper, hope kept our study group together in Church History 101, hope brought us up to, over, through the Jordan River right to where we stand this afternoon. Hope kept us close by the feet of the priests so we could cross on dry ground, hope picked us up and dusted us off when some anonymous clown pushed us aside into the mud. *But*—when we get out into our lives as ministers, we may not want to trust God with our hope; we may want a king, like the other nations. Hope can seem so impractical, and after all, the parish just started a five-year capital campaign for construction of a new congregational education building.

Yet we're going to need hope, my friends, because once you clamber up onto the riverbank beside the stones of witness, you are going to encounter the temptation to trade in your hope for a mere king; you'll feel that urge, once you get your boxes off the Hertz rent-a-camel and you get your books and clothes unpacked, you're going to climb up into your new pulpit, or your new lecture podium, or even into your comfy chair by the window, and when you look out from that exciting new vantage point you're going to gaze away to survey the prospects of exciting new fields for your ministry, and what you'll see is. . . beyond this little meadow, running along that line of trees. . . it's another river. There's another blamed *river* in the future, and now that you're looking, you can see *another* river beyond that. We've got *many* rivers ahead of us, and over the long haul, most of us aren't going to enjoy more than an occasional respite *between* rivers; often we will find that as we get further down the road, the rivers get colder and swifter and wider.

It feels like it's just not fair. Why did we spend those years in the wilderness if it wasn't to come to fair plains, fruited orchards, sunshine and relaxation? We just crossed the Jordan to come into what we've been promised. We stayed fast to the path when we were tripped up. We held fast to the promises when our brothers and sisters told us we didn't belong. We kept pressing on when the leaders of the nations attacked us. We stuck with our calling when it seemed like the waters were cheating around the feet of the priests, just to give us a chill. We spend hard years pressing on for the upward call, and when we've finally made some progress, reached a landmark, a turning point, we see more wandering, more rivers, more of the same and not an end after all.

This is a good time to remember your years in seminary which, by the time you've crossed a few more rivers, will probably look in retrospect like a May picnic catered by Amy Ehlin and her wonderful Aramark team, the cucumbers and melons, the leeks, the onions, and the garlic (well, cucumbers and melons, anyway). In retrospect, you may grumble, "Why did you call us to this ministry, when we could have stayed and had a few more bowls of soup, eaten a few more doughnuts, written a few more term papers with our friends in the ol' study group back in seminary?"

I have no word from the Lord for moments such as this, but I venture to give my opinion as one who, by the Lord's mercy, may be trustworthy. The reason we have to keep going out, the reason we always have one more river to cross, is that the good things we have built up together here are not a shrine to be venerated in immobile adoration, but are more like strong, sturdy tools to be used on behalf of a world that is still too much caught up in idle speculation, in self-gratifying indulgence, in individualistic rights, in license and exploitation, at the expense of earnest, hard-working folks who—just as we climb up on the river bank—are themselves being swept up in the turbulent flow of the surging river. We have been built together into a house of hope, a house not built with human hands. We have been built together into a house whose foundation rests not in your first ministry call or your fourth or fifth, not in the green valleys of high-steeple congregations nor in the gloom of a squalid soup-kitchen (though soup kitchens are liable to be closer than some high steeples); we have been built together into this house of hope to shelter and protect one another and our neighbors as well, and the foundation of this house rests by the side of an altogether different river, fed by the fountain of the water of life. This river of life is for nourishing and healing, not for crossing; its streams make glad the city of God, and they water our house of hope, where we behold the Lamb, our Lord. That river and that house are beyond the horizon for us now; we cannot see them yet, except by exercising the kind of hope that we learn from living faithfully with one another.

And here I offer you my understanding of the secret rationale for seminary life: for the past three years we have been teaching you not simply, not even *mostly*, the names, dates, sources, terms, and techniques that mark you as a credentialled practitioner of Christian ministry. What seminary life is about is learning a way to live every day, every challenge, every river-crossing and every pressing-on for the upward call, in the enveloping presence of the Lord our God. That's something we can't teach you one by one, on your own—we're not sending 210 Lone Rangers out there—but we teach you *together*, so that by now you know that we *all* are part of *one another's* hope: the classmates and teachers that you liked, as well as the classmates and teachers who frustrated and annoyed you. *We* are part of your hope (and you a part of ours), and in God's distinctively wry providential wisdom, some of us whom you are relieved to escape today may turn out to have spoken a word that'll be of profound help at some future, unexpected moment. We are sharers in a common hope, and partners in the obligation to bring one another across every river as best we can. God has not brought us this far to leave us; and God has not brought us this far *together* to permit us to go our separate ways. We will never let you go—and we're counting on you to hold on to us as well.

Come along, then, go out from here; but do not leave us behind. We will be with you in your study and in your social work; we will be with you at reunions, when you come back to tell us what we've meant to you and when we remind you that you mean a lot to us; above all, in the hope by which we orient all our lives, in the hope that sustains us, waking and sleeping, in the hope that leads us beyond what we can ask or imagine, we will be with you under the tree of life, built into a house of hope, beside the river of the water of life, bright as crystal, flowing from the throne of God and of the Lamb. I'll look for you there.

But for now, get away, Jordan—
   we've got work to do on the other side.

Get away, Jordan—
   we're pressing on to the upward call of God in Christ Jesus.

Get away, oh my Jordan—
   we've got to cross over to see our Lord.

EASTER VIGIL

Ezekiel 37:1-14

Prophesy to these bones, and say to them: O dry bones, hear the word of the Lord. Thus says the Lord God to these bones: I will cause breath to enter you, and you shall live. I will lay sinews on you, and will cause flesh to come upon you, and cover you with skin, and put breath in you, and you shall live; and you shall know that I am the Lord.

In the Name of the God Almighty, the Blessed Trinity— *Amen.*

    It could have been the dimness. It was awfully dark at the beginning of the service. So I may have been mistaken, but on my way in, during the processional, I though I saw... some dry bones. As a matter of fact, now that I get up here, it looks as though the whole place is filled with bones. Paula—dry bone, Jack—dry bone, Richard—dry bone, Tom, Dick, and Harry—dry bone, dry bone, dry bone. Brother Knucklebone and Sister Rib, Father Breastbone and Mother Spine, from nave to altar, from north transept to the south, choir and organist, clergy and preacher, vestry and visitors, as far as the eye can see—dry bones! So if you're a dry-boned visitor, you don't have to hide. You're welcome here, this evening, because tonight St. Luke's Parish Church in Evanston has become a whole valley of dry bones. Don't be shy; come on in, we're all dry bones here. And the word of the Lord comes to us, asking, "Mortal, can these bones live?"

    That's a tough question. Ezekiel certainly doesn't have an answer on the tip of his tongue. He's down there looking over a valley of dry bones, a valley of lifeless people. And as most preachers know, there is something challenging about standing in the presence of God and looking out over a valley of dry bones and trying to figure out what you ought to say—especially when the dry bones are somewhat comically got up in their

Sunday-go-to-meeting finery. It makes you wonder sometimes why those dry bones have dragged themselves out to the valley. Makes you wonder how all those bones got here.

It could be that here God's people tried to withstand oppression and poverty, persecution and countless other trials, that here the stress of living in a short-changed world just withered the life out of an entire congregation of holy people. Then some of the dry bones, dried up and brittle, may have been seared by the blistering heat of deprivation, by bigotry, by vicious hatred. The hatred-heated, bigotry-blistered bones of suffering and oppression have come out tonight because they know the secret, they know that here alone someone offers them precisely the same dignity that the power brokers and jet-setters get. Equal rights for all you dry bones, because God shows no partiality.

It could be that many of these dry bones have been dried out just the opposite way, by getting accustomed to the *good* things of this life. The fancy cars, the jewels, the privileges and the power steadily suck the marrow out of our bones, they rot our sense of justice and our love for our neighbors, and we gradually lose our vitality. We fatlings also fall by the wayside, we take our places in the valley of dry bones. We lose our hungry longing for God, and settle for comfort—and in less than a lifetime, we have to give up our comfort, too.

Some have been parched by poverty, some have been rotted by wealth, and some of the rest of us have just given up. Everyday plain living is hard in a complicated world like ours, and even if we never fall into the harsh extremities of poverty, even if we are never launched into the fast lane of wealth and privilege, all of us round the middle are subject to the stresses and aches, the thousand natural shocks that flesh is heir to, and even just struggling to keep in the middle can peel the flesh from your bones and leave you sitting in the valley, parched and dry and naked to the sky.

And with so many dry bones lying around this valley, I suppose we ought to consider the chance that there may have been a war here—a division in this valley, so that neighbor fights against neighbor, a struggle where everyone loses. And when the dust clears, when the conflict dies down, we don't see any triumphant forces, but just pew after pew of dry bones.

So here we all are, dry bones in collars and minks, in torn blue jeans and Air Jordans, and God's question to Ezekiel resounds in our ears: "Can these bones yet live?"

O Dry Bones, hear the word of the Lord: For those of us who have come here hungry for forgiveness and renewal after seven long weeks of Lent, I bring good news. Those weeks of self-examination and fasting have brought us here with a heightened sense of the sin that enslaves us. If you have come here with a sense of that sin, hungering and thirsting for righteousness, I bring you good news: The God who knows you and loves you knows of your sins, and God *forgives* them. God cares for you, who you are and what you do; God does not patronize you by pretending that you are not a sinner, or by offering sentimental lies about the past that has made you what you are. Lies and patronizing build the strength of evil by making sin *normal*, by suggesting that God doesn't *care* how you live your lives. But God does care—God loves you, loves your whole heart and your whole life, and God longs for you to find a renewed, stronger life in freedom, truth, love and justice. That's the meaning of God's judgment—not that God is mad at you and wants to torture you, but that God loves you so very much that God won't ignore the problems that hurt you and your neighbors. Instead, God *knows* all our past sins, God *remembers* all our past sins, and God *forgives* us. Dry bones, take flesh and live: We are forgiven!

Now, at this point I have to entertain the possibility that not everyone here has come out of an ardent sense of spiritual hunger. Some of these dry bones may have come for less exalted reasons, like peer pressure or tradition or plain arm-twisting. Hear the word of the Lord for all who have come here out from sheer force of habit: This is good! You are at the threshold of the very Lord of Hosts; you have come to the feast of Life itself. And of all the habits you could possibly have, this is the best. You have put yourself in the way of an overpowering Spirit, so that even if you are here only out of force of habit, you're in danger of being caught up and filled with a life-changing, life-giving call to *freedom* and *servanthood*. It may not sound that appealing to you now—you are, after all, *very busy* and you're here only out of habit, I remember—but by succumbing to your church-going habit, you have fallen into the habits of listening to the words of Scripture, of praying for your sisters and brothers, of taking the sacramental nourishment God offers to all the members of the Body of Christ who need to put a little flesh on their bones, and these habits have been known to lead to really time-consuming, deliberate commitments to God's ways. So if you are here tonight only because you saw the service listed in the bulletin, only because your partner dragged you, because of peer group pressure, or only because you're hoping to get a date with that really hot acolyte, you Dry Bones, take flesh and live! Your habits will be intensified and your new peer group will be the glorious communion of the saints!

And it's not only the dry bones of devout and the habitual worshippers who have come out tonight, but some bones are here for entirely different reasons. Some will be here for the exquisite music; some will be here for the glorious liturgy of the Great Vigil. If you have no intention of worshipping the Savior we praise, if you care not a whit for the Incarnation of the Living God or the Resurrection of Jesus Christ, then hear the Word of the Lord: you, too, are welcome here. God loves you and God respects your resolution to distance yourself from the Truth and Salvation that we proclaim. The God who brings life to the dry bones you see all around you, welcomes you as a *witness* to something that you will not soon forget nor will you be able to deny: you are welcome to see and remember the hope that draws your sisters and brothers to receive baptism for new life and forgiveness, the hope that draws your neighbors to this altar where we receive the bread of life and the cup of salvation. If you are dubious, if you are contradictory, welcome! The promise of God holds out to you this hope for a new and different way of living. Dry Bones, you are witnesses to the resurrection: receive the blessing of the God of Life, and bear in your hearts the memory of this hope that clothes these Dry Bones with the grandeur of the truth, with the beauty of holiness.

Can these bones live? Not by our striving, not by our pride, not by our will power or our self-denial, not by our determined believing or our desperation or our detachment. But tonight these lifeless bones will be set free, raised from sin and death into new and unending life. God will lay sinews on us, and will cause flesh to come upon us, and cover us with skin, and put breath in us, and we shall live; we shall go out to serve our needy neighbors, enemies shall embrace one another in the love of Christ, *we shall dance,* and we shall know that God is the Lord. Because tonight, lo, tonight we gather here, bleached and naked, with nothing to be proud of; and tonight, by God's love and mercy, we will go out clothed in the radiance of eternal life.